D0245857

The Art of Dress Modelling

Fashion and Dressmaking Books from Butterworth-Heinemann

Computers in the Fashion Industry   Patrick Taylor
Pattern Cutting and Making Up   Martin Shoben and Janet Ward
Pattern Cutting and Making Up for Outerwear Fashions   Martin Shoben and Janet Ward
Sew! A Complete Guide to Sewing Today   Myra Coles

THE ART OF DRESS MODELLING

MODELLING

Shape within shape

Lily Silberberg and Martin Shoben

To the memory of loving parents Isidore and Esther Silberberg

Butterworth-Heinemann Ltd
Linacre House, Jordan Hill, Oxford OX2 8DP

🔴 PART OF REED INTERNATIONAL BOOKS

OXFORD   LONDON   BOSTON
MUNICH   NEW DELHI   SINGAPORE   SYDNEY
TOKYO   TORONTO   WELLINGTON

First published 1992

© Martin Shoben and Lily Silberberg 1992

All rights reserved. No part of this publication
may be reproduced in any material form (including
photocopying or storing in any medium by electronic
means and whether or not transiently or incidentally
to some other use of this publication) without the
written permission of the copyright holder except in
accordance with the provisions of the Copyright,
Designs and Patents Act 1988 or under the terms of a
licence issued by the Copyright Licensing Agency Ltd,
90 Tottenham Court Road, London, England W1P 9HE.
Applications for the copyright holder's written
permission to reproduce any part of this publication
should be addressed to the publishers

British Library Cataloguing in Publication Data
Shoben, Martin
    The art of dress modelling: Shape within shape.
    I. Title II. Silberberg, Lily
    746.9

ISBN 0 7506 0257 0

Library of Congress Cataloguing in Publication Data
Shoben, Martin
    The art of dress modelling:shape within shape/Martin Shoben and Lily Silberberg
    p.   cm.
    Includes index.
    ISBN 0 7506 0257 0
    1. Dressmaking. 2. Tailoring (Women's)   I. Silberberg, Lily.
    II. Title.
    TT515.S55   1991
    646.4'04–dc20   91–28115
                                                                    CIP

Set by Setrite Typesetters, Hong Kong
Printed and bound in Great Britain by Thomson Litho Ltd, East Kilbride, Scotland

CONTENTS

Acknowledgements   vii

Preface   ix

Abbreviations   x

Introduction   xi

Section One   Styles   1

Principles of toile evaluation   3

Fabrics for toile making   5

Style 1   The puff ball   5
Style 2   The souffle skirt   7
Style 3   The onion or windswept look   8
Styles 4/5/6   Ethnic trousers   10
Style 7   The great knot   15
Style 8   One-piece side-draped skirt   19
Style 9   Wrap-over bias-cut dress with front drape — the Cleopatra drape   22
Style 10   Dress with handkerchief hem   25
Style 11   Asymmetrical dress with dropped waistline and circular cut skirt
             with uneven hem   28
Style 12   The threaded drape skirt   31
Style 13   Four-panelled double-circle skirt with yoke   32
Style 14   The Cha Cha frill principle   34

Section Two   Bridal Wear   35

Style 1   The souffle, made in raw silk   35
Style 2   The big bow made in dupion silk   35
Style 3   Champagne made in paper taffeta   35

Fabrics and combinations of texture   36

Bridal trains   38

Surface decoration   44

Veils   48

Section Three   Basic Skills of Modelling   51

The dress stand and modelling the toile   53

Toile evaluation   60

The principles of dart manipulation   62

The sheath dress   70

The principles of circle cutting   72

Sleeves   76

Collars   88

The simple cowl   94

Strapless bodice   96

General size chart   101

Further reading   102

List of suppliers   103

Index   105

ACKNOWLEDGEMENTS

To Alice Wright who shared her knowledge of modelling and the wonder of creating directly into three dimension with me.

To Dr James Brophy who encouraged me in turn to share that knowledge and wonder with others.

To Rita Smith, Lee Choon Leen Hoo Yum Kwong, Kim Fong Yong and Evelyn Skinner who were always willing and prepared to help.

To Jenny, Andrew and Tim Shoben, Lois Organ, Martin Day, Eric Bulmer for support, advice and help on various technical and artistic matters.

To Peter McIlvenny of Whaleys Fabrics for providing the fabrics used in this book.

To our editor Anne Martin for her patience and advice.

L. Silberberg

PREFACE

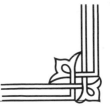

Lily Silberberg is acknowledged as the leading exponent of modelling in the country and as a long-time colleague and friend I was delighted to co-operate with her on this project. Lily was very doubtful that the tactile and creative skills of her art could be captured in a book; however, the enjoyment gained from working with her has I feel paid off and the result of the partnership is a very readable, useful and exciting illustrative record of her experiences gained over many years.

Martin Shoben

ABBREVIATIONS

CB   Centre back
CBF   Centre back fold
CF   Centre front
CFF   Centre front fold

INTRODUCTION

The beauty of this book is that it reintroduces into the fashion scene techniques that have been lost to the modern dress designer pattern cutter. Today, drafting techniques with their inherent quasiscientific theories are over-emphasized and the basic premise that clothes have to relate to the intrinsic qualities and properties of the fabrics used and the shape and stance of the figure are easily lost. Lily Silberberg's selection of clothes for this book reminds us of the halcyon days of dress design when designers had real talent and produced clothes that were an ideal marriage of fabric and wearer.

It must be emphasized that the individual styles depicted in this book should not be confused with 'fashion' but rather looked at as good examples of the principles that go to make the skill of modelling into but one successful pattern-cutting ability. There are no secrets in modelling because of its non-mechanical and non-mathematical nature. It is hoped that in time each student will develop her/his own technique which is the hallmark of freshness and individuality, a vital ingredient often missing in garments made from the flat pattern.

This book is divided into three broad sections. The first section deals with the modelling techniques for 14 dress, skirt and trouser styles. These garments have been selected because they have very strong interesting silhouettes. Some of these styles are created from pre-cut fabric lengths which when applied to the stand form the required shape. This gives rise to the title of this book, i.e. 'Shape within shape'. This first section also contains garments that are developed from lengths of fabric in the time-honoured manner. Section 2 illustrates three wedding dresses and discusses the fabrics and embellishments that went into their creation. This section also illustrates the cutting of veils and trains. Section 3 describes and illustrates skills that are needed to cut a whole range of garment styles and reveals the techniques of modelling some of Lily Silberberg's favourite designs.

It is not necessary to use this book in any special order as virtually all the styles are self-explanatory and free-standing. The keen student may well start at the beginning and work patiently through the entire book in the order that we, the authors, have determined. The book may well be used by the student or practitioner to solve certain problems or simply as a source of inspiration. Whichever way this book is used, the uniqueness of the styles and information within it will be found to be useful and inspiring.

Section One   Styles

THE PRINCIPLES OF TOILE EVALUATION

THE TOILE

The traditional way of producing a garment would be to model it directly on to the client in the couture manner. Couturiers would retain a *toile* or *muslin* for each customer which would be altered as the client changed in shape over the years. The *toile*, as it is referred to in this book, has no particular style, but contains the basic shape of the dress and must fit perfectly at all the key garment girth areas such as bust, waist, hip, neck and all the height areas such as back neck to waist and front shoulder neck point to waist and so on. This styleless shape could then be used as a basis on which to model a variety of styles. The toile is considered a very important stage in style development, and this chapter deals with the aesthetic approach to evaluating the toile.

LINE

The creator of a design must have an eye for line, and this, like most skills, takes time to develop and even then one must be prepared for unsatisfactory results from time to time. The beauty of pattern making via the toile is that the resulting effect is almost immediate and during the modelling process, flow, line and proportion can be adjusted, rather than after a pattern is made into a toile. Line, silhouette and proportion for height and girth are evident from the onset, provided that the toilist develops a discriminating eye for line. The personality of the individual will in many cases influence the outcome of the overall effect of the toile. For example, whether to overstate or understate a line or flare or to be bold or nervous in deciding the width and depth of neckline bow or drape. All of these decisions made during the creation of the toile will eventually be proved right or wrong when one stands back from the work in hand and views it from a distance or sometimes through a mirror to obtain a reverse image to provide a fresh appearance. One is then able, if necessary, to re-organize, define and refine the overall effect the design is asking for.

CONTOUR

The shape of the body contours play an important part in toile making. The medium of modelling allows for the three-dimensional aspect. One would be advised to be aware of and guided by the body contours. Very often the high points of the body, such as the bust point, the upper and lower hip, etc., will dictate the length and indeed the depth of a fold or dart. It is best to obey what the shape of the body is telling you and weave into the composition of the design that which is necessary for suppressions to obtain the desired fit. The same can be said when arranging for gathered or cut through design and one must always be aware and be prepared to adapt a design to harmonize with the contours of the body. The same must be said for the angle of darts; not only should they be used in a suppressional manner but also they must be pleasing to the optical effect of the finished garment. Although the garment may fit very well, the overall view may be marred by the visual appearance of the darts. It is best to analyse and reason as follows. Is the dart able to be incorporated into the styling features, i.e. drapes, folds, gathers? Is the dart in the correct place? Would it be better positioned in the armhole rather than the underarm? Is the dart positioned at a flattering angle? For example, on a bodice a long weak dart is less flattering than a dart that is shorter and crisper: see Figure **1**.

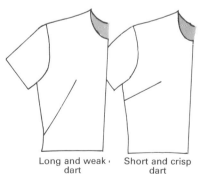

Long and weak dart   Short and crisp dart

1

SEAMLINES

The same can be said of horizontal and vertical lines of design. Horizontal lines are broadening to the figure and vertical lines are lengthening. All these factors indicate that the optical illusion is an integral part of modelling and is there to be used for the benefit of the garment design. For example, a very full-headed sleeve set into an armhole based on a full-length shoulder will have the effect of not only looking as if it is falling off the shoulder but will also have the tendency to over-balance the width of the garment at the shoulder area. To counter-balance this effect there is no harm in shortening the shoulder at the armhole, being careful to blend the line back into the armhole, (see Figure **2**). Only when one can look at the toile and say that there is no distortion of any kind within its pattern structure, fit, proportion, hang and wearability and that the toile still adheres to the original design can one say that balance has been achieved.

At no time during the modelling of a toile must one forget that the outcomes of all the effort will be a workable pattern. It is to this end that one must address the necessary accuracy. Although modelling is steeped in the artistic aspects of design, one is always testing the design as to how practical the eventual garment will be to make, albeit for couture or the mass market. To this end the toile is the pattern and within it will be found the best method of constructing the garment as the problems of construction will generally be solved during the making of the toile.

APPROACH

When first approaching a design that is to be modelled there is no formal organization as there is in flat pattern making. One can use styling tape as a guide for necklines, armholes, yokes, etc. Even then it may be found that alterations are necessary in the overall effect. It should also be noted that grain cannot normally be determined at the onset with the exception of a design that shows stripes or checks on specific angles. Only with many years of experience can it be said that in the modelling of the toile the cloth will discover its own grain in conjunction with the area of the garment piece.

Modelling is not mundane, it cannot be taught as a pure subject because it is interwoven with flat pattern cutting, grading and design. The aesthetic aspects of modelling are difficult to define. In due course the student, in the light of experience of modelling, will discover that the toile will communicate certain do's and dont's and then act and alter accordingly. In other words, the toile will take over its own creation − but only if the toilist pays attention to what is being exhibited by the toile's behaviour. Assessing the toile is no easy matter. Actually it may be wise to consult with a colleague as to the overall effect. The question is, what is right? Each person is an individual and in turn will develop her/his own eye for line and be known for that line as Dior is different from Le Croux and Hardy Amies.

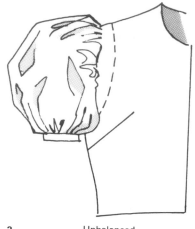

2

Unbalanced
shoulder line

Shortened balanced
shoulder line

FABRICS FOR TOILE MAKING

It is very important to select the correct fabric before starting to model on to the stand. If possible, the fabric should be relatively inexpensive and without any surface design. The choice of fabric will depend on the type of garment and should be comparable with the cloth chosen for the finished garment. It is essential to test the final garment fabric to identify its capabilities before selecting a fabric for the toile. Also at times it is advisable to select the final garment fabric for the toile particularly when making knitted clothes. The fabric selected should be easy to apply to the stand, be pliable yet stable, so that when removed from the stand as a toile there will be the minimum of stretch and distortion. Woven and knitted fabrics of various weights can be used for modelling. What follows is an analysis of the different types of modelling fabrics and their uses.

WOVEN FABRICS

Calico is the most common fabric used in modelling. It is relatively cheap and easy to handle and comes in three weights, light, medium and heavy. The choice of weight will depend on the style of the garment and the fabric it will be made in. Many of the styles in this book will require the light weight fabric as it will be easier to drape to produce specific effects.

Light-weight calico is suitable for modelling toiles for open and soft fabrics, such as crepe, heavier chiffons,

georgette, etc.

Medium-weight calico is suitable for modelling toiles of close-woven fabrics, such as satins and cottons, in fact any cloth with body.

Heavy-weight calico is suitable for modelling toiles for outerwear or any structured garment.

For materials of *intermediate weight* such as medium-weight wools a combination of light and medium calico or a layer of each could be of use. In other words the weight of the finished cloth can be imitated in the calico, to make the modelled garment more realistic.

Mull or muslin is another fabric used for modelling ultra-light-weight garments. It is slightly more expensive than calico and when unused, very stiff, although it softens up with use. Mull or muslin is very good for fine fabrics such as chiffons, organza and lace. These fabrics need more volume and very careful handling.

KNITTED FABRICS

Knitted fabrics such as cotton, wool or silk jersey come in various weights, i.e. light, medium and heavy. The very nature of the knitted stitch means that when modelling a knitted garment, a knitted toile has to be made if a realistic effect is to be produced. Jersey fabrics are generally more pliable in both warp and weft directions, coupled with the ability to be readily mouldable to the contours of the body which allows

the material to play an important structural part in suppression and tolerance.

Knitted rib

The pliability in this type of structure enables it to be very useful for the closer-cut garment. Cloth behaviour must be taken into consideration when working with ribbed knitted fabric, for example, the percentage of stretch to the square centimetre. This also applies to elasticated cloth such as Lycra. In most, but not all, cases the use of ribbed knitted fabrics alleviates the necessity for suppression for body contours. This can also be applied to garment tolerance as the knitted garment with its looped stitch will allow the body to move without the restrictions of a woven fabric.

There are occasions when materials do not lend themselves to be imitated by other cloths. In such a case, depending on the cost and availability of the cloth, it would be wiser to drape or construct the relevant areas of the garment in the 'real' material. For example, a straight dress with perhaps a cowl back, or a waterfall drape over a straight-cut skirt, could be modelled using a medium-weight calico for the straight part and self-fabric for the draped cowl or waterfall. The following 14 styles are either pre-cut 'shapes within shapes' or are developed directly on to the dress stand using the basic skills illustrated in Section 3.

Style 1. The puff ball
(Figure 3)

The puff ball skirt is cut the same shape top and bottom and the distinct puff ball effect of this skirt is achieved by draping the overskirt on to the carefully cut undergarment and the use of the darts to control the excess fullness. The unusual feature of the skirt is that it is the same top and bottom. The silhouette also lends itself to be 'souffled'. Follow the same sequence as listed below, but fix to the underlining and trim with bows, roses or other dainties.

METHOD

Pre-cut the fabric as follows
Figure 5 A−B = The length of the underskirt.
4 C−D = The length needed for the top skirt, which will depend on the weight and texture of the chosen cloth.
Calculate the material as follows:
The hip measurement × 3 is the minimum fabric required. In some light fabrics a much greater amount would be required.

THE UNDERSKIRT

1 Prepare the underskirt.
2 Ascertain the amount of 'puff' required.
3 Reduce the length of the underskirt by the amount of overhang, e.g. 10 cm from E−D (Figure 4).
4 The top cloth. Calculate the top cloth as follows:
The hip measurement × 3 by the skirt length, e.g. Hip girth = 92 cm × 3 = 276 cm. Length 55 cm plus 50 (i.e. 25 × 2) puff, top and bottom = 105 cm.
5 Use darts to reduce the top and the

bottom by 50% as in the diagram. Draw the curved darts from the cut edge top and bottom to the finished hem line and the finished waist line.

N.B. To hold the puff ball out so that it does not collapse, the fabric can be mounted over two layers of fairly firm net and made as prescribed.

This type of puff ball silhouette also lends itself to be souffled. Cut twice the length and twice the width approximately. Gather as before and fix to the underlining and trim with roses, bows or other dainties.

TO MANUFACTURE

1 Sew in the darts.
2 Trim away the excess fabric and press open the darted CB seam.
3 Gather the top waist and the bottom hem and fit them to the underskirt.

3 The puff ball

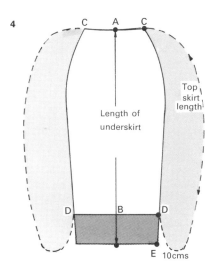

4

5 The puff ball skirt plan

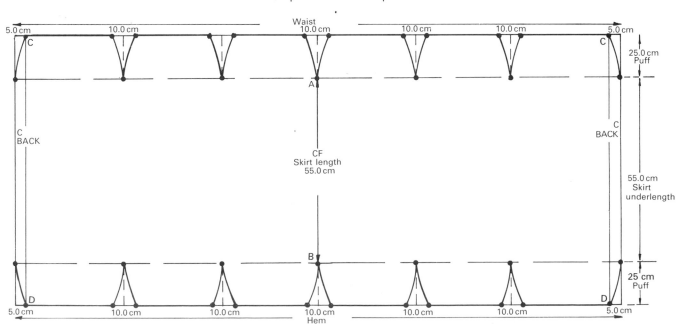

The top cloth calculation hip × 3

Style 2. The souffle skirt (Figure 6)

The souffle effect is based on the onion skirt principle. It is advisable to cut this skirt in cloth which is firm but not stiff. The effect of the skirt is best seen when light crisp fabrics are used, e.g. paper taffeta, faille, satin Dupion, organza or chiffon which has been laid over a taffeta base of the same shape, using the mounting manufacturing method. The skirt must be held out with net as for the puff ball.

METHOD

Cut the cloth twice the length of the underskirt and cut as a half-circle and then gather at the waist and the hem. The formula needed for a half-circle is as follows: Twice the waist measurement divided by 22 × 7 = the radius which is **B** from **A**. Describe an arc from **A** through **B** for the waistline.

Figure 7, the dimpled soufle effect is achieved by arranging gathered circles approximately 7.5 cm in diameter. Sew around the circles and draw them up to almost nothing. Fasten the drawn up circles through on to the underskirt and cover with roses and small bows.

circle skirt   7

6 The souffle skirt-gathered at waist and hem the fabric fixed to underskirt with roses. The strapless bodice of self or contrast texture e.g. Taffetta skirt and velvet bodice.

Style 3. The onion or windswept look (Figure 8)

Figure **8** illustrates the classic onion-shaped skirt which is shown midcalf length. This skirt has three layers; net placed on to the underskirt and then the finished fabric on the top.

Three factors create the finished shape:

1 The shortened straight underskirt lining.
2 The top skirt in fabric with wedges or darts removed.
3 Net placed between the top skirt and the lining which holds out the surface fabric.

THE UNDERSKIRT

Method

Pre-cut the fabric as follows:

1 Prepare the underskirt to the appropriate length (Figure **9**).
2 Prepare the net to the dimensions as illustrated (Figure **10**).
3 Sew the net to the top band (Figure **11**).
4 Sew to the underskirt (Figure **12**).

THE TOP SKIRT

The top skirt is calculated by formula and because it is gathered on to the underskirt it is not necessary to be too accurate in the calculation.

Top band | 15cm

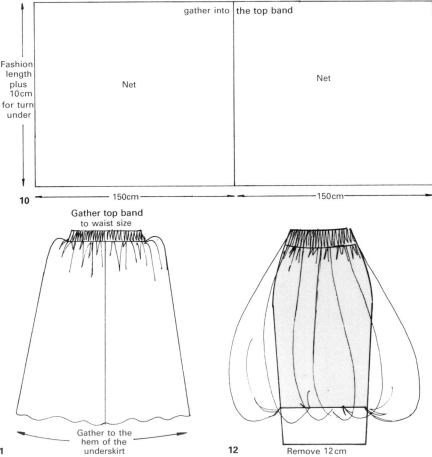

10 Fashion length plus 10cm for turn under — Net — gather into the top band — Net — 150cm — 150cm

9 Underskirt — E — 10cm — D — Reduce skirt length by 10cm

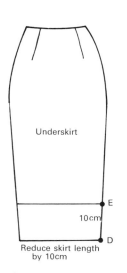

11 Gather top band to waist size — Gather to the hem of the underskirt

12 Remove 12cm

Method

1 Draw the line **A**–**B**–**C** at right angles (Figure 13). The waist measurement multiplied by 2 divided by 22 multiplied by 7 will equal the radius which is applied from point **A** to point **D**. For example:

> The waist measurement
> = 66 cm × 2 = 132 cm
> Divided by 22 = 6 cm
> Multiplied by 7 = 42 cm
> Therefore **D** from **A** = 42 cm

2 Swing arc **A** through **D** to establish **E**.
3 Swing an arc through **B** for the required skirt length.
4 Mark point **C** and **D**. The skirt is cut as for two quarters through line **A**–**D** along the centre front.
5 Reduce the hem via darts which must be evenly spaced as the diagram illustrates, to approximately half its circumference.
6 Gather at the hem and the waist to fit the underskirt.

Figure **14** illustrates the onion skirt in a striped fabric. A very pleasant effect can be achieved by cutting the skirt in four panels, see Figure **15**.

Figure **16** illustrates the twisted onion which is achieved by an eight spiral or twist to the left at the waist.

The Four Panelled Onion

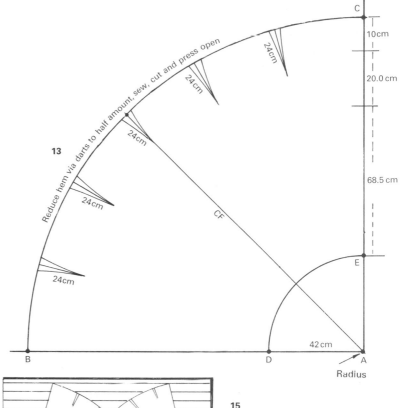

13

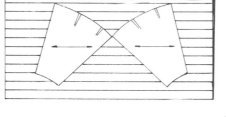

15
Fabric layout for the chevron effect

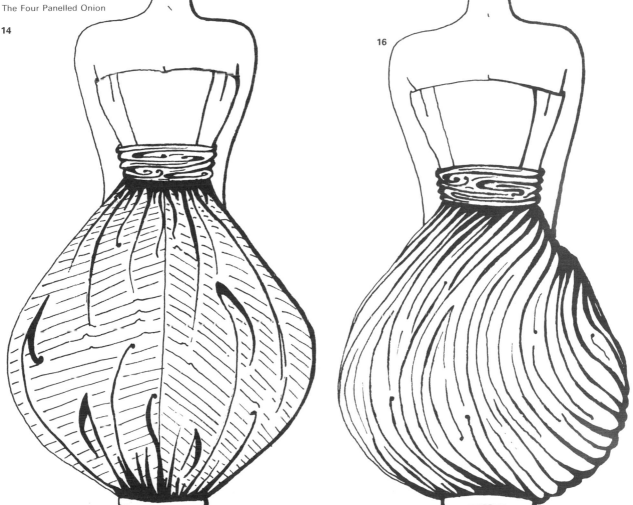

14

16

Styles 4/5/6. Ethnic trousers

The next three trouser shapes are based
on the cone and are the direct influence
of the Near to Middle East. These
garments contain the true ethnic feel,
consequently they are developed on
the flat with the built-in certainty that
the feel of drape is ever present. All
these garments are elasticated at the
waist and are designed to be pulled on
and off over the hips, therefore no zips
are necessary.

  These garments are ideal examples
of the pre-cut garment that forms shape
within shape.

THE HALF DHOTI
(FIGURE 17)

The half dhoti comes in two versions
which have a similar appearance, the
only difference being the position of
the inside leg seam.

Figure **17** Dhoti with an inside leg
seam.

Figure **18** The dhoti with the displaced
seam.

The waistband (Figure 19)

These three versions have the same
waistband which is calculated as
follows:

1 Cut the fabric one and a half times
   the hip measurement by twice the
   width of the elastic plus seam
   allowances.
2 Calculate the elastic length by
   stretching the elastic tightly around
   the hip girth.

Sewing method

1 Sew the elastic into a ring.
2 Cut the waistband casing and sew
   into a ring.
3 Place the elastic into the casing and
   sew together.

The inside leg seam dhoti
(Figure 17)

The width of the fabric should be at
least 115 cm. Soft silky fabric that will
drape well should be used such as soft
jersey or jersey single knit: whatever is
selected must be soft and maleable.

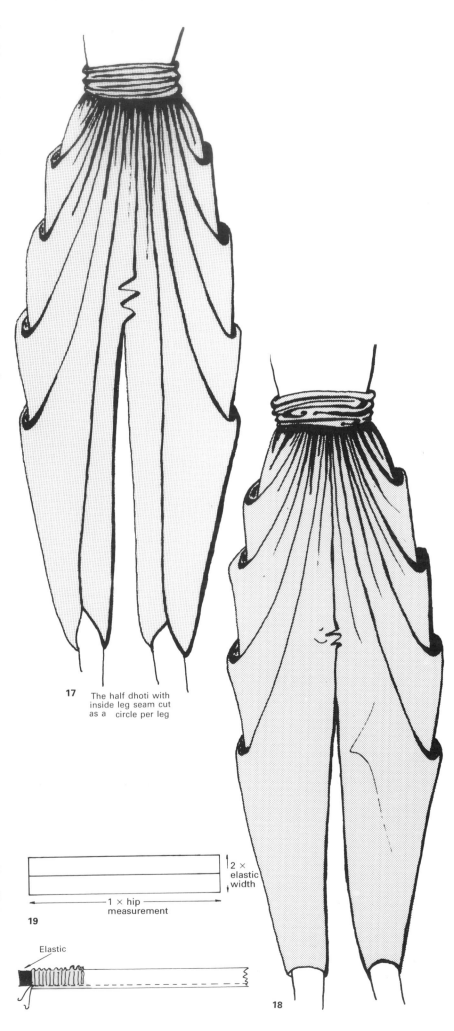

17   The half dhoti with
        inside leg seam cut
        as a   circle per leg

19   1 × hip measurement   2 × elastic width

Elastic

18

1 Take a length of fabric 114 cm wide by 120 cm in length (Figure **20**).
2 Fold the fabric locating the true bias (Figure **21**).
3 Swing an arc from **A** to **B** to establish the ankle measurement plus two turnings divided by 22 and multiplied by 14 = 15.2 cm.
4 **B**−**D** = the insided leg measurement.
5 For the body rise measurement refer to the size chart on page 99.
6 Throw an arc from the centre back through the point **F** to **G** on the fold.
7 Blend through from **H** to **E** for the front waistline.
8 Trace through **D** to **F** on to the back section (underneath). Also trace through points **H** to **G**.
9 Mark points **F**−**H**−**J**−**G**.
10 **G**−**J** = 15 cm approximately.
11 Trace through all the points.
12 Open out the fabric and cut way the excess fabric leaving 1.5 cm seam allowances (Figure **22**).
13 Fold the fabric again and stitch from **G** to **J** to form the start of the cowl (Figure **23**).
14 The distances from **J** to **E** and **J** to **F** have to be reduced to the measurement of the fullest part of the hip, e.g. by three large pleats facing towards the side seams.

20

114cm

120cm

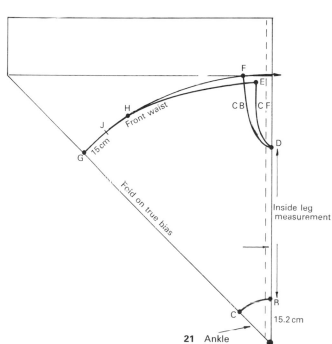

21 Ankle

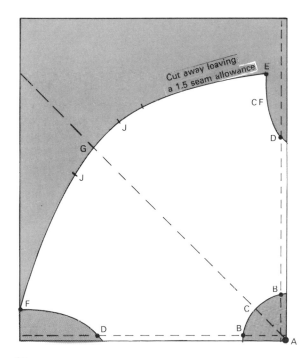

22

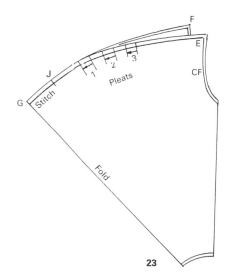

23

Dhoti with the displaced seam (Figure 18)

Follow the same construction method as the previous version with the following variation. Fold the seams inwards (Figure 24). The back waist section is much cleaner in this version, i.e. the fullness is reduced and concentrated on the side and the front (Figure 25).

Figures **26** and **27** illustrate a third style choice.

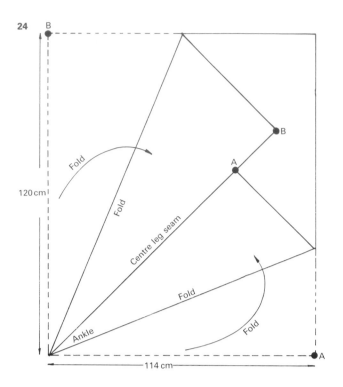

24

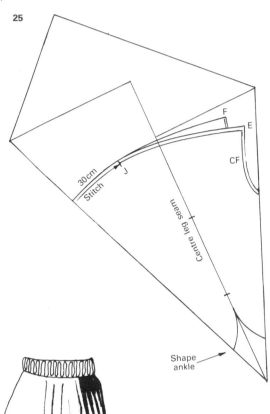

25

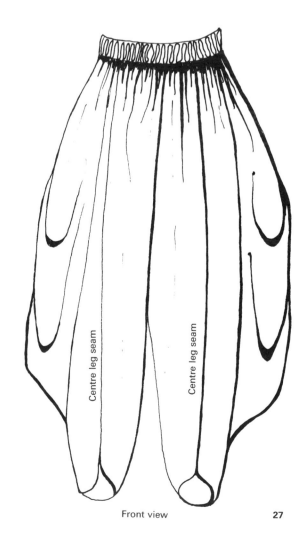

Side view   **26**

Front view   **27**

THE FULL DHOTI (FIGURE 29)

Fabric as before in texture with a minimum width or 114 cm but note that this style will need fabric in excess of 4 metres.

This full dhoti can be cut by folding the fabric as the previous dhoti; however, this method will be found to be easier to understand.

Use a large sheet of paper or draft directly on to the fabric (Figure **30**). Size 12.

1. Draw a long line and mark the centre at point **A**.
2. **A** to **B** and **C** from **A** = approximately the outside leg length. 110
3. Describe an arc from **A** through **B** to join **C**.
4. Mark point **D** at 90 degrees to line **B**–**C**.
5. Mark points **E** and **F** at 45 degrees to **B**–**A**–**C** for the dhoti fold lines.
6. **D** to **G** = approximately 32 cm for the body rise.
7. **G** to **A** = the inside leg measurement. 78 cm
8. **H** from **D** and **J** from **D** = 7 cm
9. Connect to **G**.
10. **K** from **H** = 3 cm
11. **L** from **K** = 3 cm
12. Draw line **L**–**K**–**G** for the back fork line.
13. Connect **J** to **G** for front fork.
14. **G1** from **B** = **G** from **D** = 32 cm
15. **L1** and **K1** from **B** same as **K** and **L** from **D**.
16. Mark the centre front 7 cm in from **C** for the centre front notch.
17. Add seam allowances (Figure **31**).
18. The first fold (Figure **32**).
19. The second fold (Figure **33**).

Figure **34** illustrates the two centre back notches corresponding.

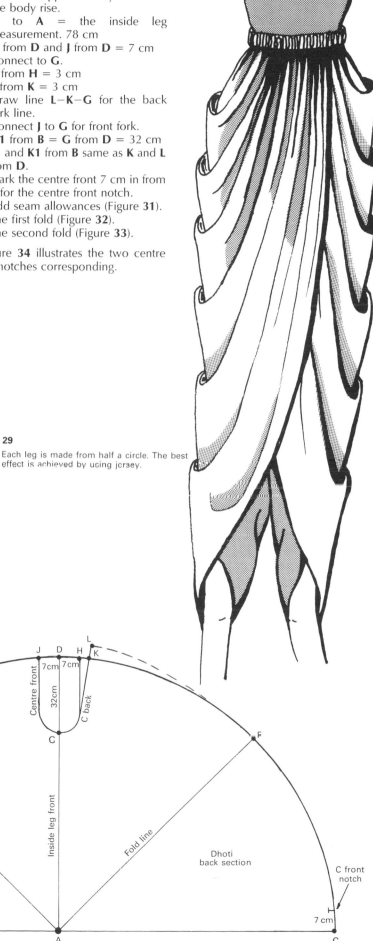

29

Each leg is made from half a circle. The best effect is achieved by using jersey.

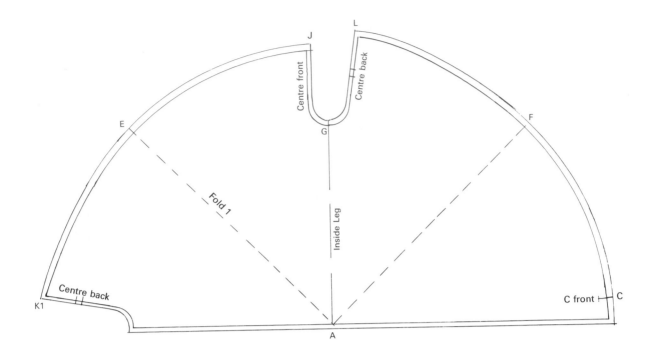

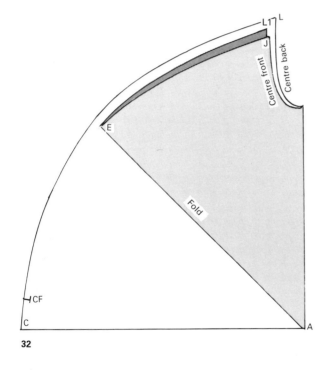

32

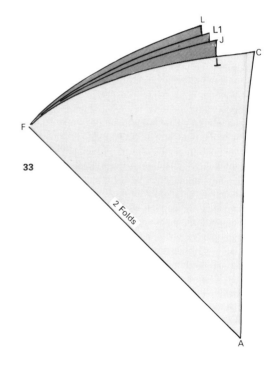

33

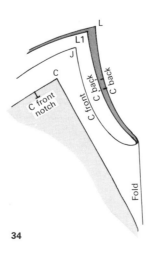

34

Style 7. The great knot (Figure 35)

This figure-hugging evening dress is one of the most sophisticated of drapes and can truly be considered a classic of its type. The choice of fabric for this garment is important. The criteria is that the cloth should be maleable, i.e. not a stubborn fabric but a fabric that allows itself to be moulded without a struggle.

This dress appears to be cut in one piece, and if done successfully, it may well bemuse the onlooker, as there should not be any visible seaming and, although asymmetrical in look, the pattern is symmetrical.

METHOD

1 Cut a large square 91 cm × 91 cm (Figure **36**).
2 Fold the square diagonally and cut along the fold. Note that the selvedge lays parallel to the torn edge (Figure **37**).

3 Pick up the top triangle and reverse it so that selvedge lays on selvedge, torn edge lays on torn edge and bias cut lays on bias cut (Figure **38**).
4 Fold again through the centre as the diagram and locate the position halfway between **A** and **B** to establish point **C**. **C** to **D** = approximately 4 cm (Figure **39**).
5 Draw an arc from **B** through **D** to establish point **E** and cut along arc (Figure **40**).
6 Open the fabric and turn back along the bias cut line (Figure **41**).

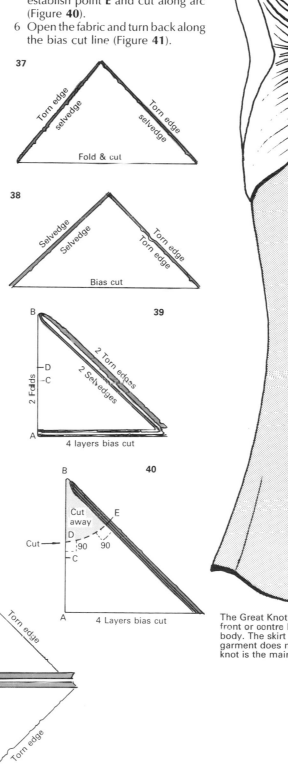

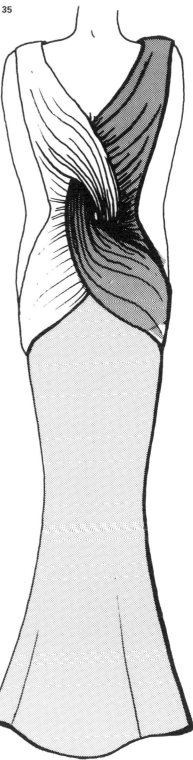

The Great Knot can be worn at the centre front or centre back or high or low on the body. The skirt goes up to the waist. This garment does not need embelishment. The knot is the main feature.

7 Turn the fabric over so that the wrong side is underneath (Figure **42**).

8 Place your hands under point D and gently gather the fabric in the hand (Figure **43**). Cross the left-hand fabric over the right-hand fabric.

9 Cross over the fabrics left over right (Figure **44**). Ensure that the fold back line is even and the drapes are even.

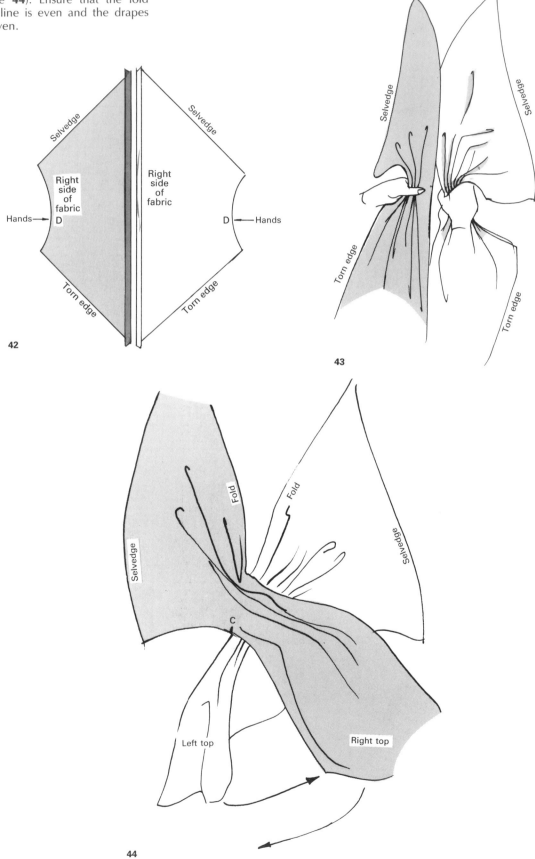

42

43

44

The butterfly stage

10 Fold again as the diagram so that the right and the left side are reversed i.e. the right top becomes the right under and vice versa (Figure **45**).

11 Pin the right bodice to the right side and the left bodice to the left side.

12 Decide the position of the centre front and place on to the dress stand and decide the cross-over point at the centre front (Figure **46**).

13 Use the seam at the waist approximately to pass away unwanted fabric.

14 Model away freely until the required tension of drapes is achieved.

15 Clear away the excess length of the side seam by nipping in and moving towards the waist region (Figure **47**).

Figure **48** illustrates the finished fitted shape.

16 To ensure that the waist seam is invisible, mark the seam line under a horizontal fold.

17 Place three balance marks (Figure **49**).

18 Remove the toile from the stand and select the better side to pattern and mark up (Figure **50**).

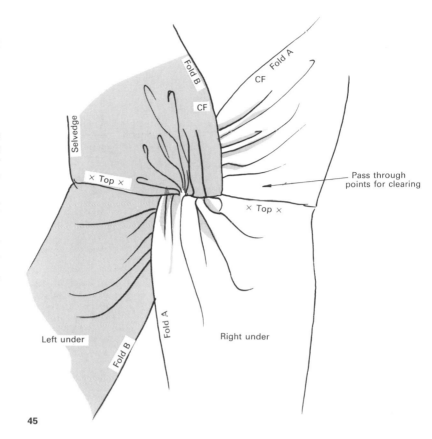

45

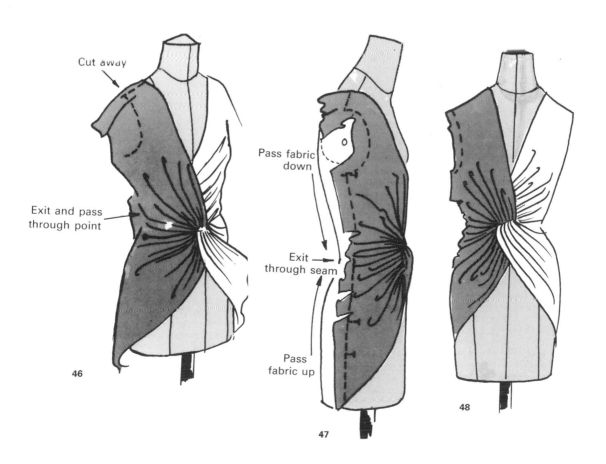

46

47

48

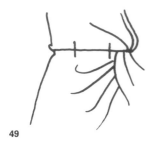

49

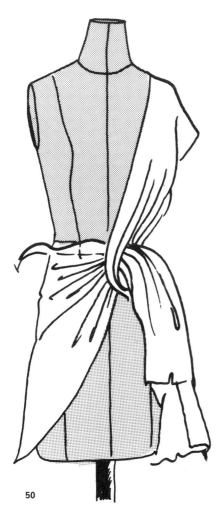

50

19 Side A, neaten from point 4 to
point 4, and then assemble as follows (Figure **51**).

THE HOLE

Assembly

1 Leave an opening between point 4
and point 4 to pass through the
other side bodice (Figure **52**).
2 Neaten between point 4 and point
4.
3 Join points 3 to 3, 2 to 2 etc., and
sew on the inside.
4 Cut side B.
5 Neaten between points 4 and 4 and
thread through the hole.
6 Sew points 4 to 4, points 3 to 3 etc.
7 Finish by sewing the left side seam.
8 Note that the right-hand seam at the
waist will tend to point upwards
whereas the left-hand side seam will
face downwards.

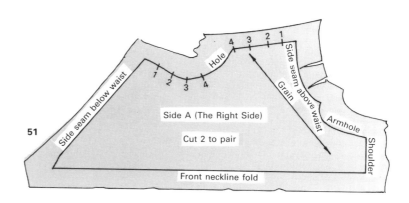

51

Side seam below waist

Hole

Side seam above waist

Grain

Armhole

Shoulder

Side A (The Right Side)

Cut 2 to pair

Front neckline fold

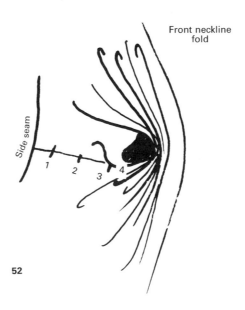

Front neckline
fold

Side seam

52

Style 8. One-piece side-draped skirt

This brilliant draped skirt could be cut in one piece if the fabric is wide enough (Figure **53**).

METHOD

Use an existing basic block-type skirt pattern.

1 Take a large section of fabric approximately 91 cm square (Figure **54**).

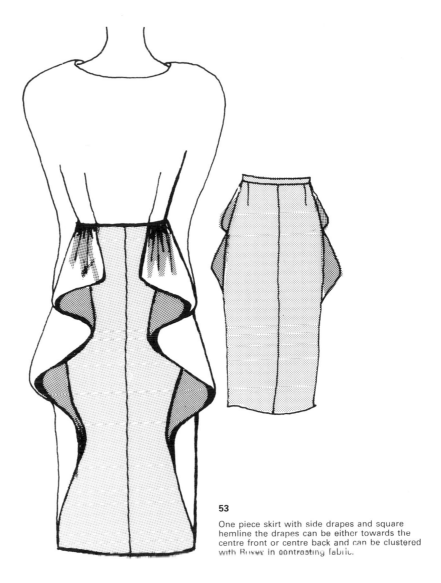

53

One piece skirt with side drapes and square hemline the drapes can be either towards the centre front or centre back and can be clustered with Roses in contrasting fabric.

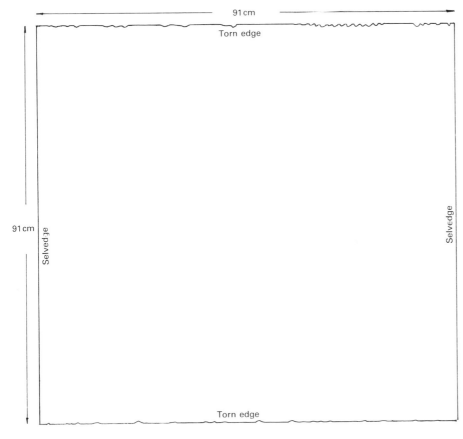

54

2 Fold the fabric as the diagram, off laying the centre back seam by 2.5 cm (Figure **55**).

3 Lay the front skirt block on to the torn edge of the fabric and mark around the skirt pattern (Figure **56**).

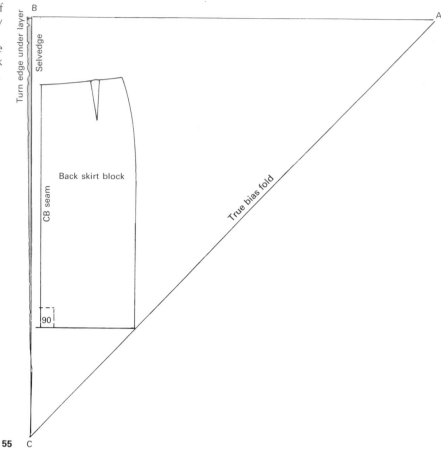

55

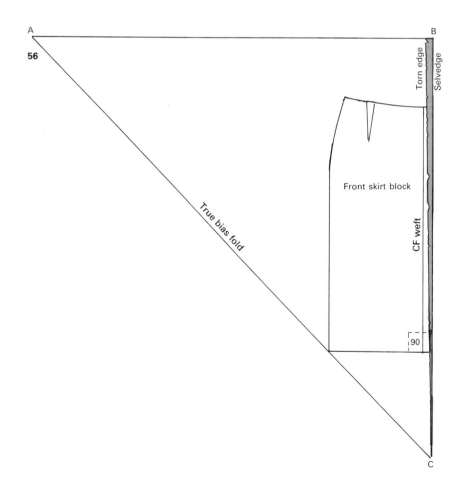

56

4 Turn the fabric over and use the back skirt (Figure **57**).
5 Cut away the shaded areas (Figure **57**).
6 Fold the side seam for fold 1 (Figure **58**).
7 Continue folding as the diagram and trim away the top waist edge (Figure **59**).

Figure **60** shows the finished folded pattern, opened out.

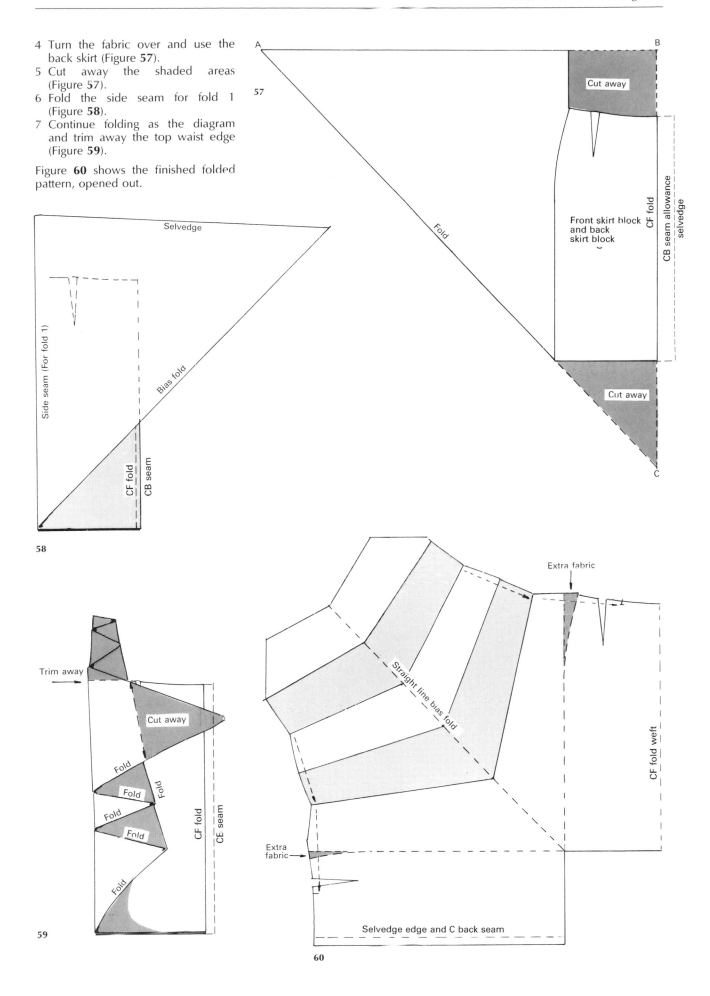

Style 9. Wrap-over bias-cut dress with front drape — The Cleopatra drape

This drape needs a fabric with a maleable spongy quality, e.g. moss crepe (Figure **61**).

Estimate the width and length of fabric needed. If, while modelling, the fabric proves too narrow, add extra fabric on to the original piece. The final garment may well need to be modelled in a wider fabric.

Note that, although this garment is symmetrical it will need to be modelled as a whole dress. Half the dress is modelled with the fabric folded and then finally opened out.

62

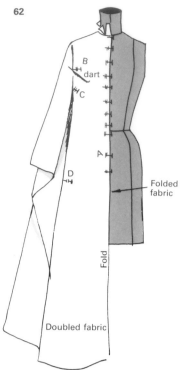

METHOD

1 Take a viable length of fabric, i.e. 1.5 m.
2 Fold and mark the centre front with finger pressed crease (warp).
3 Place the folded fabric on to the stand and pin frequently down the centre front to the upper hip (point **A**) (Figure **62**).
4 Allow the fabric to hang gently from **A**.
5 Pin the bust suppression into a dart at **B**.
6 Place a pin **C** at the underarm point.
7 Pin **D** just above the hipline to hold the fabric into position (Figure **63**).
8 Feel for the hip and cut into the area above the drape area.
9 Pick up drape at point **E** from point **D** and pin into position (Figure **64**).
10 Repeat this by cutting into **F** at the side seam and lifting up the fold at the centre front (Figure **65**).
11 Pin into position.
12 Repeat for third fold to establish point **H** (Figure **66**).
13 Trim away unwanted fabric at the side seam.

61

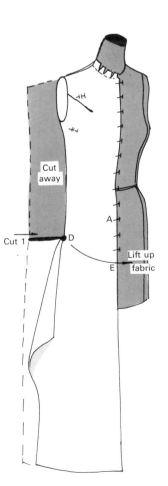

The Cleopatra drape. The body work is cut in one piece and looks superb in undecorated fabric to enchane the simplicity of the drape at the centre

63

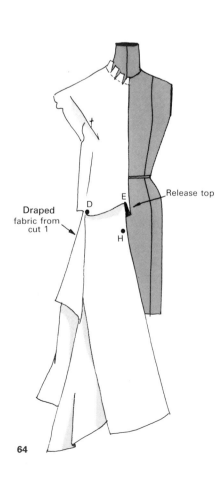

64

The diamond inset

1 Decide on the position of the diamond inset and mark points 1/2/3 (Figure **67**).
2 Lift up the centre front section as diagram (Figure **67**).
3 Curve a line from the centre front to the hem.
4 Add a section of fabric at hem if required.

The sculptured stage

1 With the fingers locate the centre front and pin down to the hem (Figure **68**).
   To sculpt the waterfall, estimate as follows:
   K to **L** is the first drop
   L to **M** is the second drop
   M to **N** is the third drop.
2 Cut the shape of the draped waterfall (Figures **69** and **70**).
3 Check waterfall drop and adjust if necessary (Figure **71**).

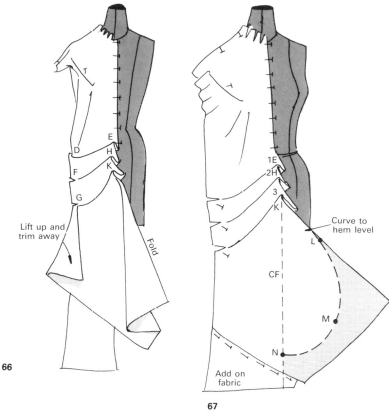

66

Lift up and trim away

Fold

67

Curve to hem level

CF

Add on fabric

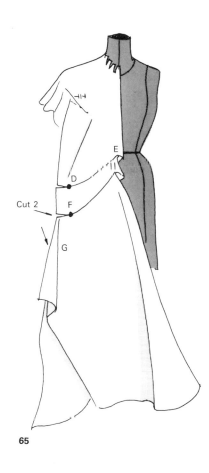

65

Cut 2

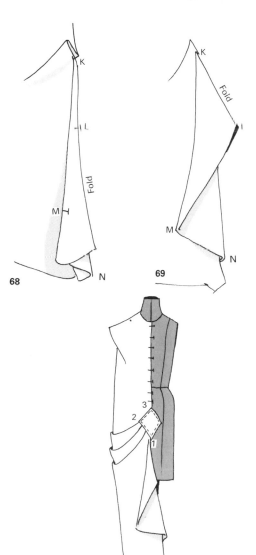

68

69

71

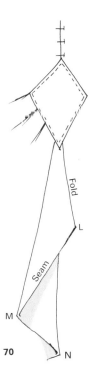

70

Fold

Seam

The kite shape tab

1 Cut the tab long and wide enough to cover the drapes, which will be applied to the lining.
2 Cut kite shape to cover the hole caused by the centre drapes.
3 Remove the patch and cut into the folds to create the kite shape (Figure **72**). Figure **72 (b)** shows the kite shape cut in lining with balance marks indicating drape positions.
4 Pin the kite shape on to the dress stand (Figure **73**) and mark all points.
5 Carefully remove the toile from the stand.

Figure **74** illustrates the folded toile, and Figure **75** illustrates the final opened toile.

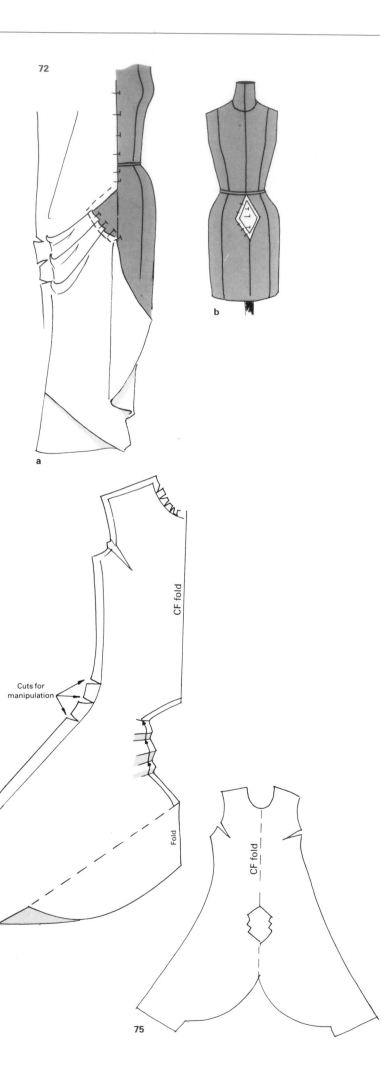

Style 10. Dress with handkerchief hem (Figure 76)

This semi-fitting dress has a very attractive pointed hemline hence the name handkerchief and was very popular during the 1930s. The pointed hem is achieved by cutting into the side seam and pivoting the cut line downwards into the hem. The cut is then covered by a decorative inset patch of fabric (front and back).

METHOD

The front

1 Clear the selvedge by folding in about 4 cm.
2 Apply the fabric to the centre front of the stand and pin into position (Figure **78**). Make sure that the shoulder neck point is covered.

At this stage the neckline can be provisionally scooped out; a more accurate stylish neckline will be developed at a later stage.

3 Provisionally trim the neckline as the diagram (Figure **78**).
4 The new neckline may not lay close to the body (Figure **79**). If not, follow this remedy.
5 Release the fabric at the shoulder by removing the shoulder pin. Smooth the fabric upwards to remove excess fabric at the neck (Figure **80**).
6 Smooth fabric across the bust point with the flat of the hand and support with a pin at the underarm point (Figure **81**).
7 Pin a dart from the underarm to the armhole to the bust point (Figure **82**). The fabric at the side seam should not be stressed.
8 Determine the side seam. From **A – B** is straight, as a semi-fitting dress the waist is not discernable (Figure **83**).
9 Use judgement to place an arc of pins that correspond to the style feature at the side seam (Figure **84**). Pin **C** is positioned just below the waistline. Imagine the arc as a mirror reflection to judge the size, position and depth of the arc on the finished double-sided garment.
10 Cut down parallel to the side seam until opposite pin **C** (Figure **85**).
11 Follow the pinned arc top in **E** getting progressively closer. If the fit at the waist needs increasing, readjust the pins (Figure **86**).

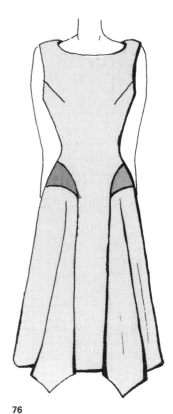

76

Handkerchief points, insets are to cover side holes. Insets can be embroidered, see through lace etc.

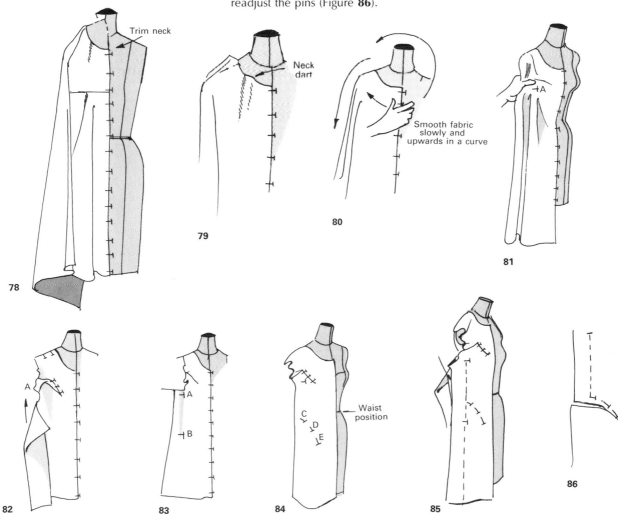

Trim neck

78

79

Neck dart

80

Smooth fabric slowly and upwards in a curve

81

A

82

A

B

83

C
D
E

Waist position

84

85

86

12 Open the cut and project the fabric into the hem (Figure **87**).

13 Mark point **F**, which is the site of the next pivot point (Figure **88**). Cut and pivot down from **F** for the second flute.

14 Determine a line just above the cut and design your line (Figure **89**).

15 Cut a piece of fabric that will cover the open cut and pin over the cut (Figure **90**).

16 Mark off the hole and draw over the pins to trace the design line on to the inset piece (Figure **91**).

17 Turn under seams on the inset piece and repin into position (Figure **92**).

18 Figure **93** illustrates the front view. Identify the side seam lenghts.

19 Let the fabric relax into several fullnesses.

20 Cut excess fabric away from the side seams.

21 Place a pin **Y** on the cut side seam roughly the same level as the centre front (Figure **93**).

22 Place pin **X** below **Y**.

23 Pick up line **X−Y** and cut along line **X−Y** and allow the fabric to drop (Figure **94**).

24 Retain the pin in the side seam (Figure **95**).

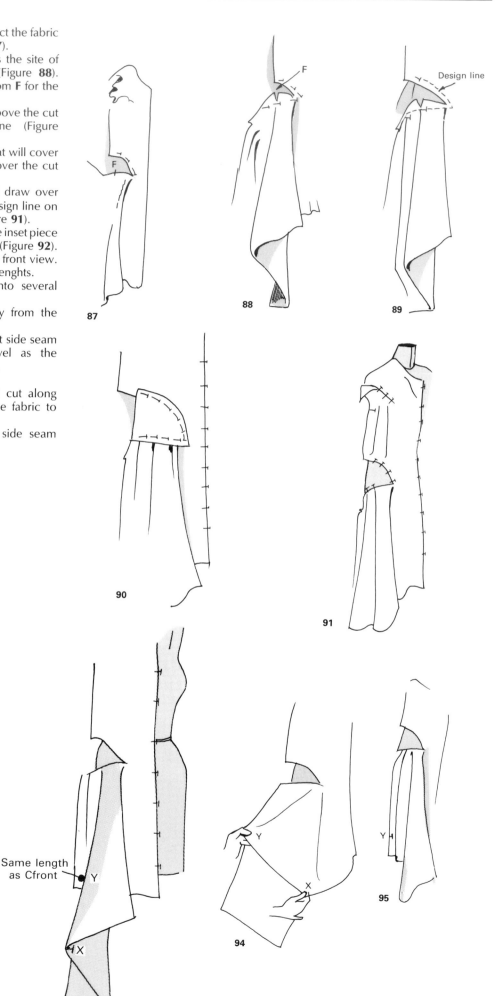

The back

The back of the dress is achieved in a similar manner to the front.

1 Prepare the selvedge and place the fabric on to the back of the stand (Figure **96**).
2 Swing the dart into the shoulder and trim away the back neck.
3 Prepare the side seam to accept the cut (as the front of the dress) (Figure **97**).
4 To carry on the design line from the front so that it harmonizes from front to back, provisionally pin the upper side seams together (Figure **98**).
5 Critically examine the line running from the back and front and adjust if required. Place pins **H**−**J**−**K**.
6 Cut open line **H**−**J**−**K** as the front (Figure **99**).
7 Remove pin and pivot the fabric down into the hem as the front (Figure **100**).
8 Marry up the side seams by locating the front side seam position (Figure **101**).
9 Readjust the side seam (Figure **102**).
10 Trim the side seams and mark the back and front. Establish the corners and cut as the front hem (Figure **103**).
11 Patch in the back cut by preparing the inset as for Figure **90**.
12 Close the garment at the shoulder.
13 Mark the back and front remembering to mount the back shoulder over the front.
14 Pin the neckline with a smooth line over the shoulder (Figure **104**).
15 Mark the armhole.

Style 11. Asymmetrical dress with dropped waistline and circular cut skirt with uneven hem (Figure 108)

Before commencing to model this dress, plan the style features on to the dress stand with pins as indicated in Figure **109**.

The drapes located around the waistline area will affect the upper part of the garment so it is essential that a lining pattern is cut according to the planned neckline (see Figure **110**) and that this lining is applied to the dress form before the fabric is applied. This will ensure stability to the finished garment.

1 Look at the working drawing and plan out the half neck and armhole using either pins or styling tape (Figure **108**).
2 Cut a back and front facing for the armhole and the neckline which will be used to contain the adjusted asymmetrical fabric to be bagged out when sewn (Figure **110**).

METHOD

Cut a section of fabric, 91 cm in width, which is long enough to cover the stand from shoulder to 20 cm longer than stand. Place the fabric, selvedge way down, lightly over the dress stand and place pins to steady the fabric (Figure **111**). Place the fabric two-thirds to the right-hand side and one-third to the left.

The left-hand side neckline

1 Cut from the shoulder down in the direction of the centre front leaving a seam allowance above the planned neckline (Figure **112**).
2 Remove the temporary pins and smooth the fabric backwards to clean and clear the neckline of bubbles (Figure **112**).

The suppression

1 Place a pin into the shoulder and note the superfluous fabric at the armhole (Figure **113**).
2 Cut gently into the bubbles and release them (Figure **114**).
3 Smooth the superfluous fabric downwards into the general direction of the hem (Figure **114**).

108

Asymetric hem, flounces are circular cut and gathered. Side embelishments can be roses or bows, pearls or sequins etc.

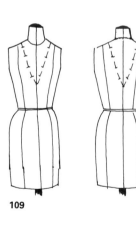

109

110

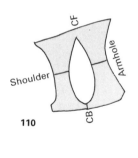

111

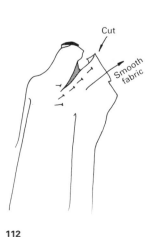

112

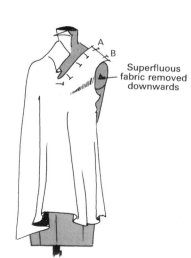

113

114

The side embellishment and drapes

Pivot the fullness draping from the bust point into a sympathetic line to form a side drape (Figure **115**).

Right-hand side of the neckline

1 Tighten the right hand side of the neckline by repinning the neckline so that it lays on top of the underfacing and therefore achieves a symmetry with the left-hand side (Figure **116**).
2 Mark the neckline through (Figure **116**).
3 Lift up the fabric from the bust point (BP) for the second drape. Note that at this stage both bust points have been accommodated with suppression in the form of folds (Figure **117**).
4 Cut into pin **D** (Figure **118**).
5 Look to see if the fabric is indicating where it should be picked up (Figure **118**).
6 Lift up the fabric over the left hand to allow extra length in the top edge of the fold (Figure **119**).
7 Feel down the side seam and position a pin just above the waist (Figure **120**).
8 Cut into the pin in the general direction of the side seam to release the fabric (Figure **120**). The main objective is to remove the source of the folds from the side seam so that it is a smooth uninterrupted line and will contain more length.
9 Carry on pinning at the side seam, cutting into the pins and picking fabric to achieve the required radiating folds (Figure **121**).
10 Adjust the left-hand side to ensure that the folds are clean and are performing as required (Figure **122**). Concentrate on the inset piece line where the line will be visible.

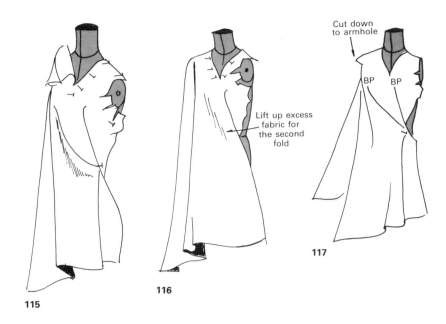

Lift up excess fabric for the second fold

Cut down to armhole

BP BP

117

116

115

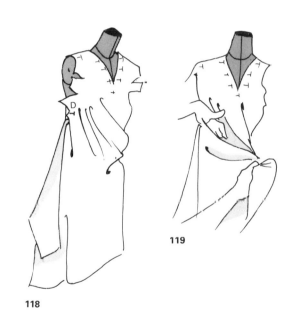

D

118

119

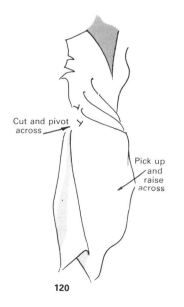

Cut and pivot across

Pick up and raise across

120

121

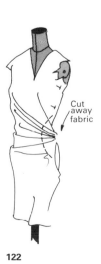

Cut away fabric

122

The embellishment

The side seam embellishment will be cut on the bias so that it moulds to the body.

1 Use pins to plan the style line and adjust the folds if they are not evenly spaced (Figure **123**).
2 Cut into the side seam and raise into position.
3 Use pins to plan design line **G**—**F** (Figure **123**).
4 Cut the fabric away below the style line leaving a generous seam allowance (Figure **123**).
5 Model the back body as for the one-piece fitted waistless dress with a centre back seam (Figure **124**).
6 Place a section of fabric over the side style line to mask in the hole. Using a pencil, mark over it tracing through the style line (Figure **125**).
7 Turn in the seam allowance and evaluate the shape (Figure **126**).
8 Evaluate the toile and adjust the radiating folds (Figure **127**).

The double-circular-type skirt

1 Cut two squares length by width and cut them into circles using the methods described on page 70 (Figure **128**).
2 Cut the point out, leaving the required length, e.g. cut out the inner circle which will be applied to the style line (Figure **128**).
3 Shorten one of the circles as Figure **128**.
4 Apply the two circles to the style line **F**—**G** (Figure **123**).
5 Make the two circles up as one unit and apply together (Figure **129**).
6 Repeat the circular process on the back skirt (Figure **130**).

Marry the sides seams and join the shoulders as for previous exercises.

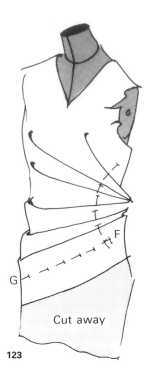

123

Cut away

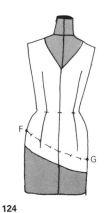

124

125

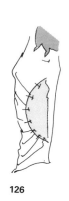

126

127

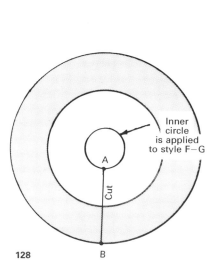

Inner circle is applied to style F—G

A

Cut

128   B

129

130

Style 12. The threaded drape skirt

This skirt is a variation of the draped skirt with waterfall. In this particularly stylish variation the drape hangs from a vertical band. Although it gives a 'one-piece appearance', the drape is a separate inset (Figure 131).

METHOD

1 Return to the stage indicated by Figures **333–335**.
2 Rearrange folds at **B** to give greater and even spaces (Figure **132**).
3 Cut down line **A–B** and allow the material to drop (Figure **132**).
4 Raise the fabric so that **A** overlaps **B** and forms a small dart. This dart allows a degree of suppression from hip to the waist (Figure **133**).
5 Pin line **C–A/B** (Figure **133**).
6 **D–E** becomes the other side of the dart (Figure **134**).
7 Determine the waist and the hip by feeling through the calico to the stand (Figure **134**).
8 Cut away the fabric parallel to the waist and down the side seam (Figure **134**).

Figure **135** illustrates the drapes entering the band. Readjust the folds if necessary, especially around the side suppression area.

The drape insertion

1 Transfer markings of the established skirt drape across the band by placing of pins into line **A–D** (Figure **136**).
2 A quarter-circle insert is used for the drape. Prepare a circle by referring to page 70 on circle cutting.
3 Derive a ¼ circle from a square of fabric the appropriate length (Figure **137**).
4 Apply the drape to the vertical band until length **AB–C** relates to the skirt **A–C** (Figure **138**).
5 Fold the quarter-circle and place the folds to correspond to the folds on the skirt band, i.e. **G–G** and **H–H**, etc. (Figure **139**).
6 Cut down the inside fold of the dart **E–D** and open up the dart and then thread the drape through to correspond with the established skirt drape (Figure **139**).
7 Replace the dart over the drape (Figure **139**).
8 Continue working on the drape to give the required line and direction (Figure **140**).

Cut a curved line at an angle for the front fold. Figure **141** shows the finished folded inset.

131

Threaded through separate side drape.

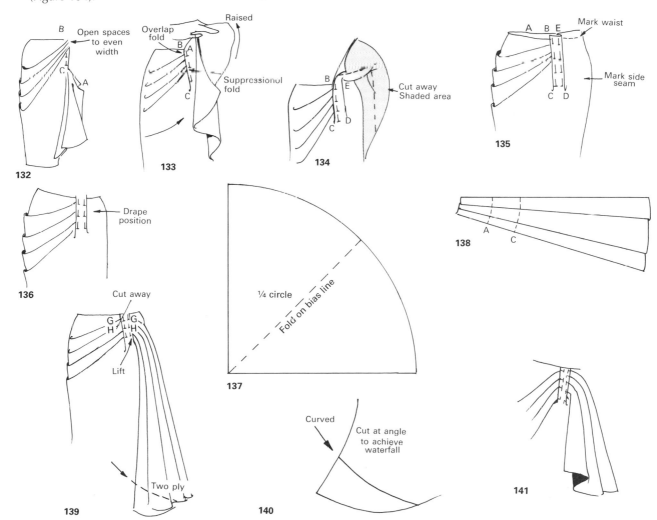

Style 13. Four-panelled double-circle skirt with yoke

This skirt is tightly fitting to just below the upper hip (Figure **142**).

METHOD

The yoke

1 Fold a section of fabric. The dimensions are the depth of the required yoke depth by a quarter of the hip measurement (Figure **143**).
2 Apply the folded fabric to the dress stand and cut in and down to the waist as the diagram so that the fabric moulds around the body (Figure **144**).
3 Repeat this process until the fabric fits as required around the body (Figure **145**).
4 Trim away the excess fabric above the waistline (Figure **146**).
5 Place cross pins at the required site of the design points and use style tape to plan the required style lines (Figure **146**).
6 Cut away the excess fabric and add seam allowances (Figure **147**).
7 Remove the yoke from the stand (Figure **148**).
8 Trace the yoke to the other side of the body and repin to the stand.

142
Four panelled double circle skirt with fitted yoke

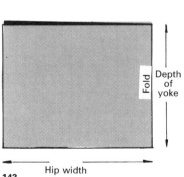

143

Fold

Depth of yoke

Hip width

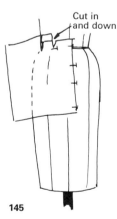

Cut in and down

145

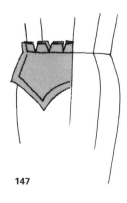

147

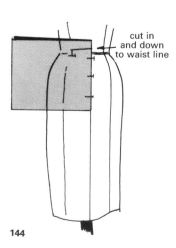

cut in and down to waist line

144

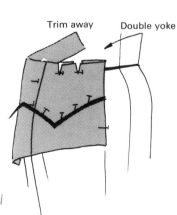

Trim away   Double yoke

146

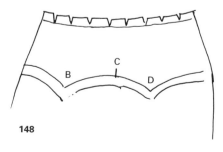

B   C   D

148

The skirt

1 Calculate the length of the skirt by holding the fabric to the stand:
A−B = the skirt length;
B−C the distance around the points to the centre front (Figure **148**).

Figures **149** and **150** illustrate the fabric corresponding to the yoke measurements.

2 Apply **C−E** (Figure **150**) to the centre front of the stand and pin as the diagram (Figure **151**).
3 Pin the fabric around the curve (**C− B**) cutting and pivoting to project the fabric into the hem (Figure **152**).
4 Pin down on to the skirt stand.
5 Level the skirt (Figure **153**).
6 Repeat the technique for the other four panels (Figure **154**).

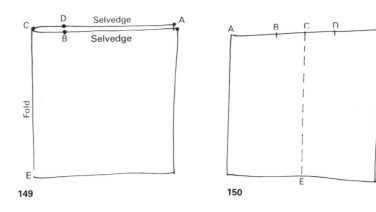

149　　　　**150**

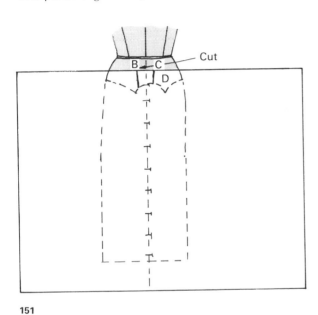

151

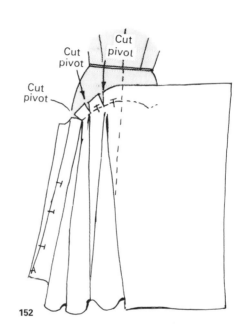

152

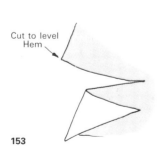

153

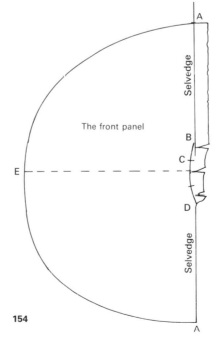

154

Style 14. The Cha Cha frill principle

This effect is bold and unsophisticated and can be applied to either the upper part of a dress as a sleeve or to the hem to form a silhouette suitable to the popular Cha Cha dance (see Figure **155**). The effect is achieved by gathering strips of contrast or 'self' fabric on to a rectangular lining base and then gathering the rectangle to the armhole or hem as the case may be. Almost any spiky fabric will be suitable for this effect, especially a metallic gold or silver lurex. Tafetta or a crisp silk will also be ideal. This effect in suitably tasteful lace can also be used for bridal wear.

METHOD

The cha cha sleeve

Figure **156** shows the lining mount. Select a suitable fabric, either see-through or fine crispy net.

1 Cut a lining approximately 60 cm × 30 cm plus seam allowances.

2 Mark up the fabric as indicated: **C–D** will be the underarm length; **A–B** will form the top of the sleeve; **A–C** will finally be gathered into the armhole. Strips will be applied to **E–E**, **F–F** etc. The seam allowance added to **D–D** will be turned up to form a casing for the elastication used to grip the sleeve to the upper arm.

3 In the main contrasting fabric cut 12 crossway strips 7 cm wide.

4 Sew two strips together, gimping the edges and gather through the centre of the strips to 60 cm.

5 Make a ring casing for the elastic to fit the upper arm.

6 Sew each gathered strip to the lining base along the lines **E–E/F–F** etc. (Figure **157**).

7 Fold the fabric lengthwise and, with the sewn frills inside, sew the underarm length, i.e. **C–D** (Figure **158**).

8 Insert a gathering thread into line **A–B** and reduce to 6 cm for the top of the sleeve (Figure **158**).

9 Turn the sleeve through to the right side and reduce area **A–C** to the required armhole size (Figure **159**).

10 Insert the ringed elastic (Figure **159**).

11 Apply to the armhole of the garment (Figure **159**).

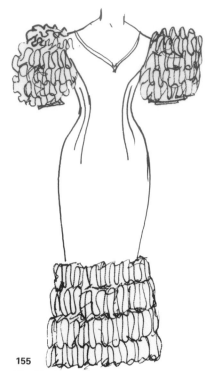

155

Cha Cha Sleeve
Frou Frou can be of contrast fabric and texture. For example the body in velvet and the Frou Frou in organza or taffeta. The same effect can be used with great effect at the bottom of the skirt.

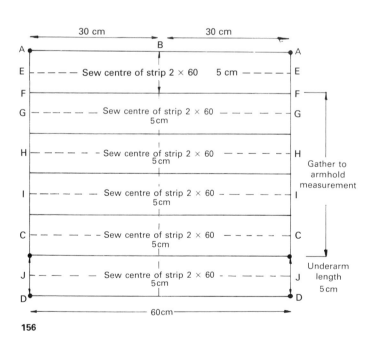

156

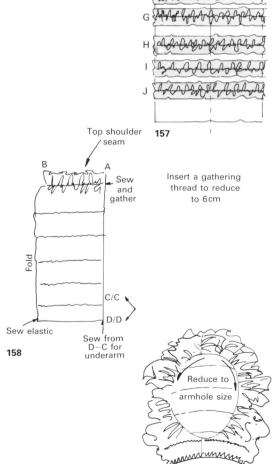

157

Insert a gathering thread to reduce to 6cm

Top shoulder seam

Sew and gather

Fold

Sew elastic

C/C

D/D

Sew from D–C for underarm

158

Reduce to armhole size

159

Section Two   Bridal Wear

Bridal gowns come in a variety of silhouettes, shapes and proportions and are in many respects the pinnacle of the modeller's art. To most women it is to be the most important — certainly the most memorable — garment of their lives. These three gowns are made in the finest silks and have very strong, elegant and beautiful silhouettes which are decorated with roses, lace and pearls. The skills, ideas and inspiration for designing, modelling and making these garments can all be found in the sections devoted to skills and styles. A careful analysis of each of these three garments will reveal the wide exciting variety of silhouettes, fabrics and textures, sleeve confections and concepts, surface decoration and trains and veils that can be found in the classical and modern bridal dress. Read on for a full analysis of each garment.

Style 1. The souffle made in raw silk

Looking at the three very individually designed gowns in this book, it is easily seen how each garment contains strong individual ideas. For example, Style One, when viewed straight on from the front, only hints at what is happening to the garment from the back. It is only when the garment is viewed from the side that it can be seen that there is harmony in this contrast of a rather flat uncluttered classic-cut front combined with the richness of a sculptured integral train overlayed with a wealth of fabric held in place with roses. The bodice of this gown is cut with a simple

drop shoulder and a wide but shallow neckline and is in effect shoulderless. The straight-cut rather severe collar-cum-sleeve effect not only helps to frame the neckline but also acts as a very good receptacle for more roses which in turn softens the whole effect.

Style 2. The big bow made in dupion silk

Again we see a classic uncluttered overall silhouette of an A-line skirt that falls from a demure bodice waist. The bodice is only a vehicle for the ball sleeve which is in proportion to the rest of the bodice by virtue of it not being overwhelming and made even lighter by the application of lace flowers and leaves sewn on with tiny pearls. When viewed from the side, the train, which is an integral part of the back skirt, does not start abruptly from the front but the side seams without impinging on the flow. Overlaying this train is a second train depicting a dramatic bow and ends draped so that the bow and ends become as one. Again, the proportion of such an addition to the garment must in no way overwhelm but on the contrary enhance the movement and flow of the overall effect. Lace, too, has been added to the overtrain, again in as light a mode as possible. This has been done to mask a seam in the bow ends that was necessary because of the width of the fabric used. Nevertheless, the effect has, if anything, added to the overall effect of the garment.

Style 3. Champagne made in paper taffeta

When analysing a design it is wise to attempt to render it down to basics, in this case, a simple strapless bodice, surmounting a simple straight skirt. In effect, these two elements are the wearable parts of the gown, the rest is superimposed. To juxtapose the starkness of the straight skirt, cowles have been hung from the centre front looping at the side and disappearing around the back under the train. The bodice is a basic strapless one which has been overlayed with fine piece lace, then beaded and pearled to give an otherwise rather solid appearance a certain lift. The scalloped edge to the top and waist of the bodice is effected by simply using the edge of the lace in appliqué to these areas and outlining with two rows of pearls. The sleeves which are not strictly sleeves are based on a triangle — the long bias edge folded as for the lattice sleeve, then modelled on to a shaped shoulder strap which is helpful in itself as bodice support. The train of the gown is applied as an entity of its own. The bodice and the skirt are separate, only coming together at the end via the waist — the skirt has its own petersham — so that it sits into the waist. The train is fixed on to the back skirt waist so that at no time is there any strain or pull on the bodice but all the stress is taken by the waist of the garment.

All three styles are shown in the plate section.

FABRICS AND COMBINATIONS OF TEXTURE

The overall effect of these three garments is due to the interaction of sophisticated cutting and draping and the visual beauty of the fabric combinations and textures. The following fabrics were used for the wedding dresses to emphasize and add to their intrinsic qualities.

Raw silk or *wild silk* has an easy flow and drapes boldly. It is firm to handle and is closely woven. Many people are put off by this fabric because of its rough texture. The fabric is mostly imported from the Far East and woven by hand and contains bars, slubs and what would be termed flaws in other more refined fabrics.

Dupion silk has an easy flow and a good bold drape. It is firm to handle, close woven and more refined and smoother to the touch than raw silk. The fabric exhibits a lustre in sunlight, but is otherwise muted.

Both raw and dupion silks are prone to crumple. However, these creases fall out in a very short time which makes the fabric an ideal choice for a wedding dress. The fabric is also light in weight and can be bought in some twenty colours.

Paper taffeta can be either silk or acetate. The behaviour of this fabric is depicted by its name, 'paper'. Closely woven, smooth and light in texture, the overall effect of the garment is crisp and will, if allowed, tend towards the angular. Although light in weight, the fabric has a certain stubborn resistance and has to be coaxed to drape, but once in place, the effect is delightful and opulent.

All of these garments were mounted on to nylon lining, because nylon does not crush and is generally stronger than acetate. Also nylon holds its shape better and does not allow the silk to flatten. In some cases, polyester satin linings were dropped in for a smooth inside finish.

There are many other fabrics equally fitted for wedding gowns. Whichever fabric or combination of textures are chosen, it should always be borne in mind that this gown is a very special garment for a special occasion. Because of the formality of a wedding, the garment will bear a stamp that will be very hard to alter for further use at other occasions. Whatever colours the gown is dyed, however much it is shortened, it will always look like a dyed shortened wedding gown. The following fabrics and their characteristics provide an alternative to the fabrics used in the photographed wedding dresses.

Duchess satin

This has a luxurious but dull sheen with a heavy rich, smooth, creamy texture. It is more inclined to billow than to drape. It is easy to handle because of its close weave. This type of fabric lends itself to be used for a more classic uncluttered style of gowns rather than the fussy and frilled type. It can be of silk, acetate, a combination of both or polyester.

Slipper satin

This is much lighter in weight but usually with a shiny smooth texture. It is not as easy as Duchess satin to handle, because of the inclination to pucker during seaming. This fabric drapes very well and has good moulding qualities when cut on the bias (as above for quality).

Lace

Lace comes in various qualities and types.

Guipure, not strictly a lace but rather an embroidery, can be bought and used as a piece or cut into motifs and spread, depending on the effect required. This type of bold lace combines very well with fabrics such as raw and dupion silks and duchess satin and can be purchased in various qualities, i.e. cotton, acetate and rayon.

All over lace (piece lace) is often manufactured with scalloped edges. It is very easy to handle on its own but depending on the weight of the lace, it is more advisable to back this type of lace on to net if it is to be used as a see-through area of the garment, if not mounting the lace directly on to the base fabric is very effective. A lace of this variety that is made of closely constructed but individually clustered subjects such as flowers, scrolls or leaves can be cut into individual clusters and reapplied in required areas of the garment (see page 35). These are not sewn down but are applied by sewing beads or pearls on to the centre of the leaf thereby giving a lighter overall appearance.

Windows
The lace motif is positioned in the required place; it is then closly sewn to the body fabric, and the body fabric is cut away so that the lace becomes a 'see-through window'.

SLEEVES AND CONCEPTS

Bridal gowns can be, and often are, made or marred by their sleeves. Proportion should dictate the size, but once an eye for proportion has been developed, among the first things that one becomes aware of are the sleeves. The other strand to this awareness is taste. For example, a design that contains a crinoline silhouetted skirt with a train comprising overlayed frills, lace and bows surmounted by a plunge neckline bodice with top-heavy leg-o-mutton-type sleeves is indeed not to everyone's taste! But this is a word picture of a design shown in popular magazines dealing with weddings. In the recent past a bride married in a church was obliged to have her whole arm covered, and the neckline had to be modest. This has to a great extent been allowed to lapse, but one still finds that perhaps 75% of wedding gowns still adhere to the long sleeve. On the other hand the remaining 25% of manufactured wedding gowns show a variety of arm coverings ranging from very brief top arm covering to the most elaborate of puffed sleeves interlaced with gupure lace motif windows attached to the armholes with bows and roses. Trains too are a part of wedding heritage if not folk law. Apart from the cost of fabric, the length and width of a train should be studied with regard to the building (e.g. width of the aisle) in which the ceremony will take place. A train some twelve foot long and eight foot wide could somewhat overflow in a small parish church but look quite modest in a cathedral. Another aspect of the train is that if it is applied, it can also be made removable, if required later in the day. A garment with a built-in train of course does not allow for this.

THE PLANNING AND MAKING OF A BRIDAL DRESS

The planning and making of bridal gowns, be they for couture or the mass market, places the onus of responsibility on the person who makes the toile. It is through their gift that the ultimate effect will be seen in the eventual garment. It is for them to be aware, not only of what the garment will be like when not in motion, but also how the garment moves, how it holds together with its surroundings, how it will travel (hopefully without crushing) and still keep within the costing allowed. In all my years of 'bride watching', I have still to see an ugly bride or one that did not glow on her 'day'.

BRIDAL TRAINS

FABRICS

Trains are a splendid addition to the back view of any wedding dress. The longer the train, the more impact the wearer makes on the audience. When considering the making of a bridal train it is necessary to use fabrics at least 150 cm wide so that seams to increase the width of the fabric will not become unsightly. If narrower fabrics are used the toilist should use discretion and place the seams in an inconspicuous position.

Trains are very effective if used in firm bold types of fabrics such as duchess satin, paper taffeta, moire or wild silk and in lace organza placed over lining then backed with fabrics as above. Soft fabrics such as crepe or slipper satin will not have the required texture to give the train the importance it deserves. Note that to stiffen up the fabric it is suggested that a firm net be used. Never use fusible interlinings as they will inhibit the fabric's natural characteristics.

The actual dress can be of either fabric or lace and either straight cut, i.e. empire line, or full-skirted.

SILHOUETTE

The design of the dress will not be affected by the train as most emphasis is placed on the back view. Be adventurous and adaptable; do not restrict these effects only to wedding dresses; made in smaller dimensions they can be most effective in evening wear. The effects illustrated in the following pages have been sculptured and created flat on a surface, then hung on to the finished garment to adjust for gravitational pull; this approach is pure modelling with the pattern piece being the outcome of the work, and is a tripartite approach as it integrates the three most important factors in modelling, i.e. concept, cloth and technique.

See plate section.

THE DETACHABLE TRAIN (FIGURE 160)

Method

This train is created on a flat surface rather than the stand. Prepare the fabric, in this case 150 cm wide, and even then it may be necessary to join the fabric beforehand or even after the train has been modelled to make the joins less conspicuous.

1 Take a large square of fabric 150 cm × 150 cm (Figure **161**).
2 Fold the fabric into a triangle with the bias in front of you. Locate point **A** by measuring down from the centre back and estimate that position on the fold of the cloth. Place a pin into point **A** (Figure **162**).
3 Hold point **A** firmly (Figure **163**).

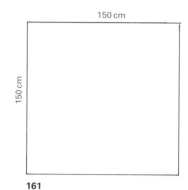

161

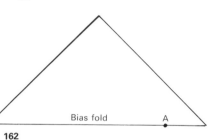

162

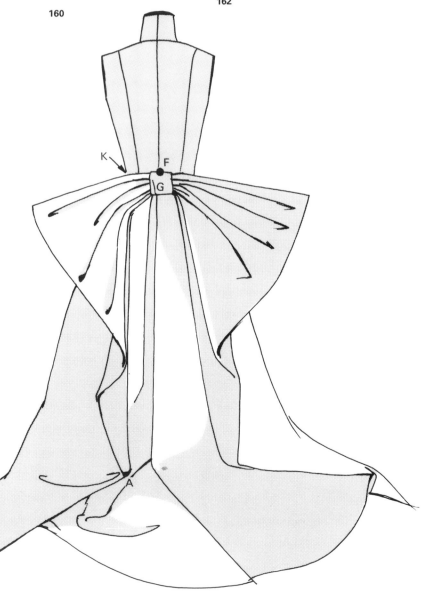

160

4 Lift up the top layer about 35 degrees from point **A**. Fold as the diagram (Figure **164**).
5 Estimate the width at the bottom of the bow ends, e.g. **B**–**D**. Fold the remainder under to obtain the required visual effect. Place pins under fold **E**–**A** to pevent slippage (Figure **165**).

Formulation of the bow
1 Fold down line **F**–**E** (add on any section that needs extra fabric) cut away the folded area under section **F**–**E**–**C**.
2 Bunch up three folds between **G**–**G**–**G**; these three folds will be marked in with the applied knot (Figure **166**).

3 Figure **167** illustrates the unpleated bow. Curve **F**–**E** as required.
4 Prepare a knot from a small rectangle and mark in the folds (Figure **168**).

To displace seam line D edge (Figure 169)
Return to Figure **165**. Turn the whole bow over and crease the fabric on the finished edge. Cut away unwanted fabric, see Figure **169**. Decide on the finished new seamline (which should be positioned out of sight) and replan the seam. Neaten under the bow, adding and taking off fabric as necessary. Position on the dress stand to check the finished proportions.

1 Pick up a fold at **J** (see Figure **166**) and bring it around into pleasant folds.

2 Repeat this by cutting two patterns to pair and arranging them on to the dress stand either above or below the waist (Figure **170**).

KITE-SHAPED TRAIN

Figure **171** illustrates the kite-shaped train which is the centre structure that fits behind the bow and ends developed earlier. To cut this, measure **K**–**D** on Figure **172**. Cut a rectangle measuring **K**–**D** in length by 150 cm in width. Cut diagonally from **K**–**D** (Figure **173**). Reverse **K**–**K** to achieve a kite shape.

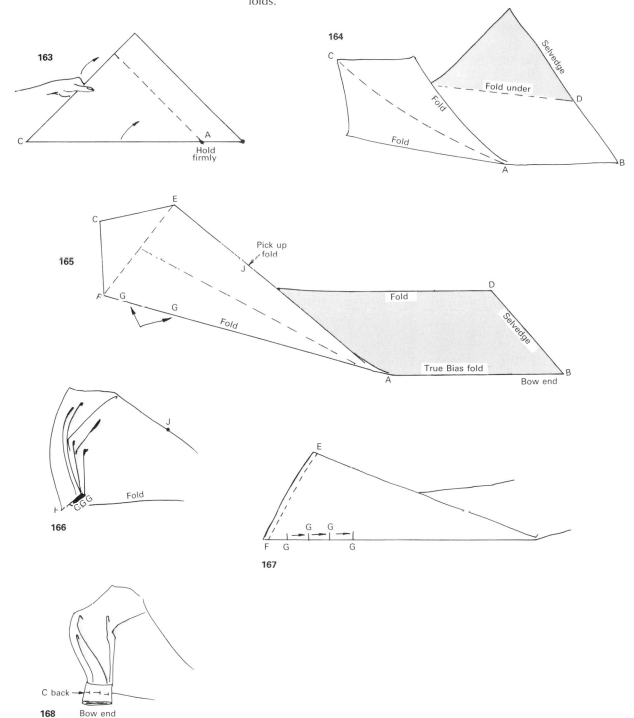

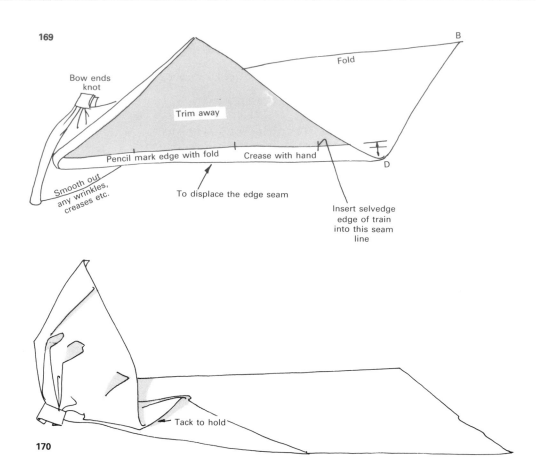

169

Bow ends
knot

Trim away

Fold

B

Pencil mark edge with fold

Crease with hand

D

Smooth out
any wrinkles,
creases etc.

To displace the edge seam

Insert selvedge
edge of train
into this seam
line

Tack to hold

170

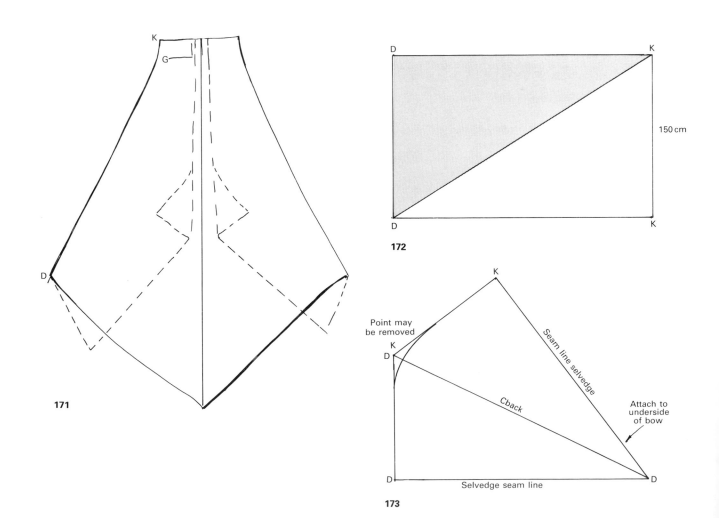

171

K

G

D

D

K

D

K

D

K

150 cm

172

K

Point may
be removed

K

D

Seam line selvedge

Cback

Attach to
underside
of bow

D

D

Selvedge seam line

D

173

Attaching the bow

Feed the kite-shaped train into the seam that was displaced in Figure **169**.

Shaping the train

1 Position the kite-shaped train under the bows into the seamlines. To adjust the centre back seam, study the garment from the side view.
2 Hollow or scoop the centre back seam if required (Figure **174**). Also, if necessary, open up the centre back seam at the top of the train and fill with extra fabric so that the train is extended in width and will not pull and bunch as the bride moves forward.
3 To extend the train at the centre back length, follow Figure **175** and extend as desired.

COMBINED TRAIN AND BOW (FIGURE 176)

The objective of this style is to create folds, therefore no true measurements can be stated. However, the areas marked are suggestions to be used as guidance.

Fabric required is 150 cm wide by 250 cm long.

1 Cut the fabric diagonally as the diagram and discard the unwanted section (Figure **177**).
2 Mark point **A** (Figure **177**).
3 Fold **B1** to **B** (Figure **178**).
4 Fold **C1** to **C**.
5 Fold **D1** to **D**.
6 Cut from the centre back inwards through the folded pleats until **D**1 is reached. Stop, lift upper layer of fabric and continue to cut through

the inside fold, so that the bow fabric can be worked independently from the drapes. Point **B** will become the new centre back.
7 Fold from **B** along **E**, which is the proposed centre back line.
8 To sculpt the outer edge mark the flat folded toile as follows: Draw line **E**−**F** which is a continuation of **B**−**G**.
9 Measure **F**−**G** and apply to **H**−**J** minus approximately 4 cm.
10 Locate **K** which is on a straight line between **G**−**J**−**K**.
11 Mark with a pencil.

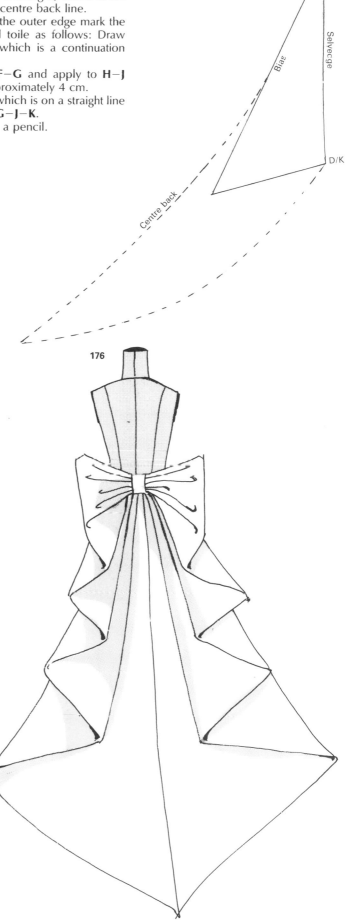

175

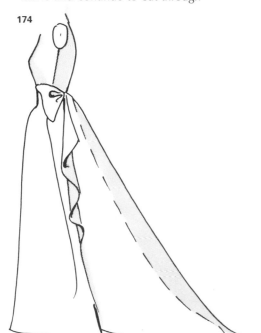

174

176

12 Open out the fabric and cut through
    from **E** to **F** through **J** and on to **K**,
    then stop and trim off unwanted
    fabric to form an ellipse (Figure
    179).

    Figure **180** shows the draped train.

The bow (Figure 181)

1 Extend the centre back line upwards
   approximately 5−6 cm for the flat
   undersection of the bow.
2 Draw line **L**−**M** at 45 degrees from
   the centre back plus turnings.
3 Cut away shaded section. The
   gathered end of the bow which
   reverses on to the surface is
   approximately 30 cm.
4 Mark point **N** which is 30 cm from
   O.
5 Draw curve **O**−**N**.
6 Cut in at **N**.
7 Fold **O** to **L** and pleat in **N** to **O** into
   L−**B** into three upward facing bold
   folds.
8 Cut a gently curved line from **N**−**K**.

   Figure **182** shows the finished side
view of the train and bow.

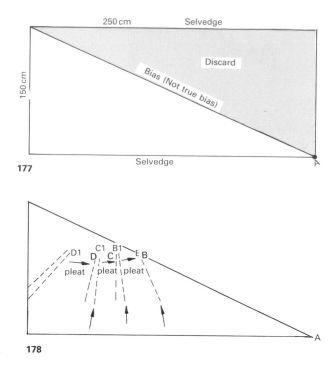

177

178

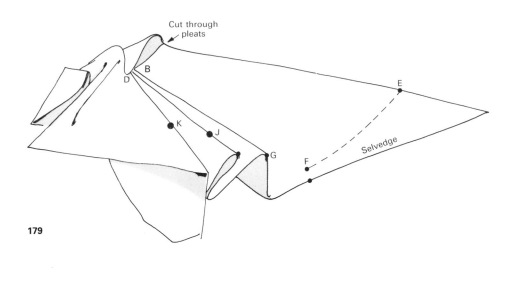

179

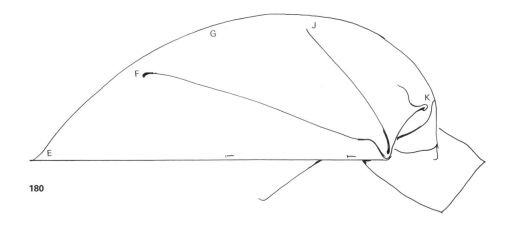

180

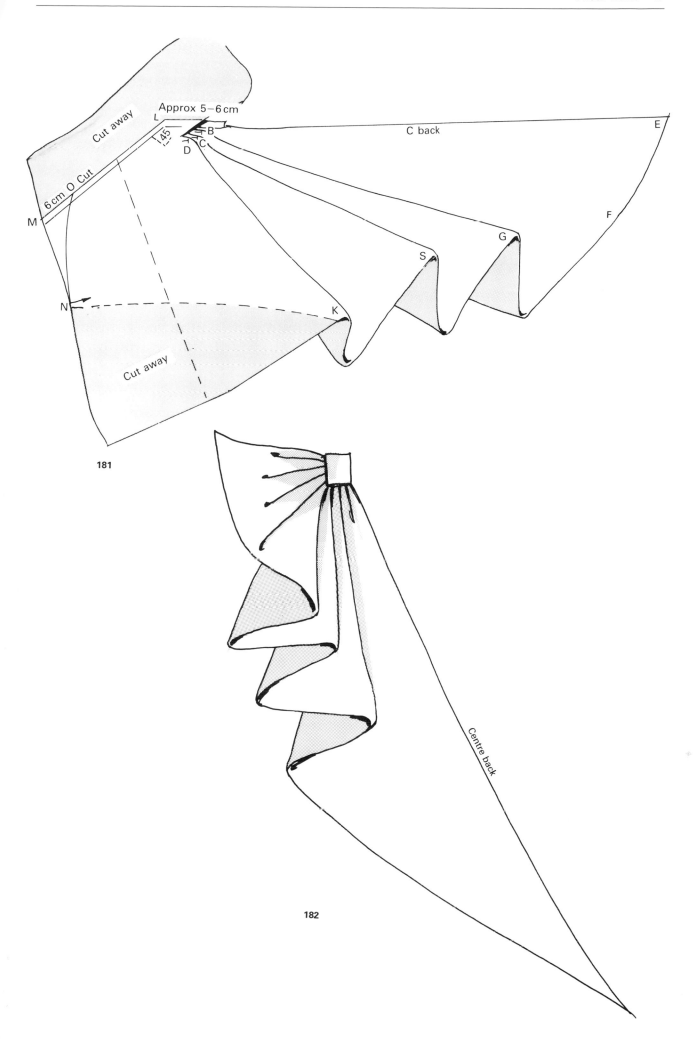

Cut away

Approx 5–6 cm

L

45

B

D C

6 cm O Cut

M

C back

E

F

G

S

N

K

Cut away

181

Centre back

182

SURFACE DECORATION

This chapter deals with the small embellishments that are added to the finished garment. The embellishing of the wedding gown depends to a great extent on cost. But when arranging for trimmings, be it beading, appliqué flowers or bows, research must be done into the compatability of the trimmings with the garment fabric, otherwise the garment may very well suffer during cleaning or washing because the trimmings are contradictory.

BOWS

Although simple in appearance, a bow can positively enhance the entire appearance of a dress. It can be positioned at the neckline, the waist or hem and can be a solitary bow or one of many. Bows can be made in contrasting or 'self' fabrics and can also be decorated and embellished with sequins and pearls. The following diagrams illustrate the techniques of modelling the two basic bow categories, which are the *flat bow* (Figure **183**), the simplest of shapes consisting of rectangles cut to the required size, and the *three-piece bias-cut bow* (Figure **184**). This bow is in many respects far more beautiful than the flat bow and can be used to embellish and adorn the finest wedding or evening dress.

The flat bow

Method (Figure **185**)
1 Cut a rectangle twice the finished loop size doubled and double the finished width plus turnings.
2 Fold on centre line, right side inwards.
3 Stitch and turn along the long edge.

Note that bow ends can be added if required.

The three-piece bias-cut blow

This bow reduces bulk by gathering the top layer of the bow on to a flat underlayer.

Method

1 Take a square of fabric of the required size (Figure **186**).
2 Fold the square diagonally. *Do not crease* (Figure **187**).
3 To gather the fabric, spread the fingers out a short distance up from the point (Figure **188**).
4 Slide the index finger under the fabric fold, two fingers above until you arrive at the loop length desired (Figure **189**).
5 Fold the fabric under into a loop. The dotted line will be folded back to establish the width and shape of the bow points (Figure **190**).

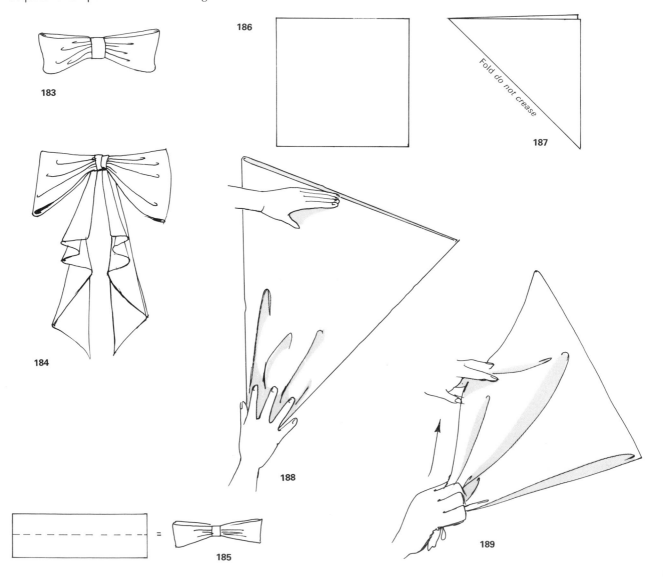

6 The top bow folds are created by drawing the fingers together and lightly clustering the cloth, keeping the left hand as a weight (Figure **191**).

Figures **192–194** show the finished bow shapes. See also plate section.

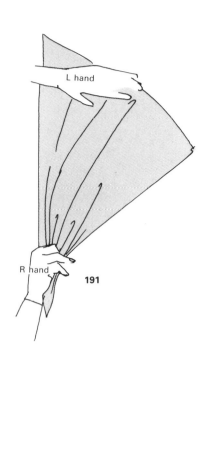

191

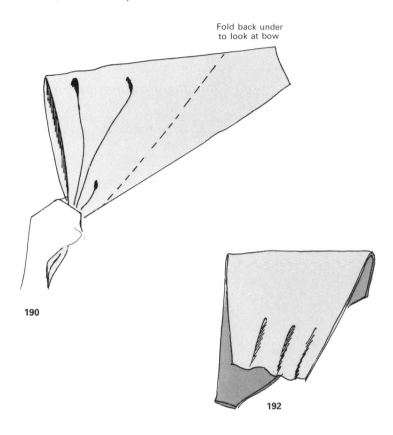

Fold back under to look at bow

190

192

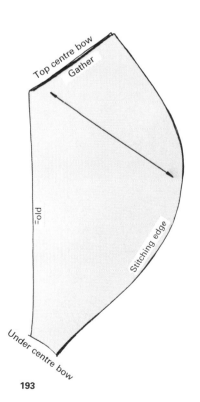

Top centre bow

Gather

Fold

Stitching edge

Under centre bow

193

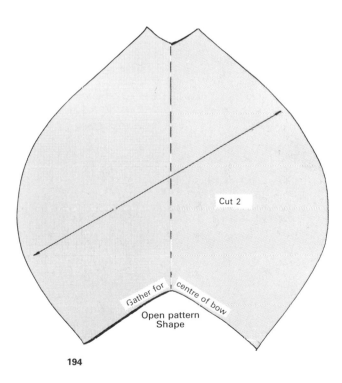

Cut 2

Gather for centre of bow

Open pattern Shape

194

Sequence of assembly

1 Fold on the centre line, right side inwards.
2 Stitch outer edge **A**–**B** and turn through.
3 Pull through on to right side of fabric and underpress to pair.
4 Gather the long open edge and fold over to meet the short open edge.
5 The knot is a rectangle cut on the bias.

The ends

The ends have to give the appearance that they are an integral part of the bow and that the bow has been casually tied a moment before. The reality is that the ends are carefully and separately cut and fastened securely behind the bow.

1 Cut a length of fabric selvedge way down. The dimensions will be twice the finished length of the ends by half the finished length in width (Figure **195**).
2 Plan a suitable curve and cut from **C** to **B** (Figure **196**).
3 Holding **A** with the index finger of the left hand, lift point **D**, approximately one-third and arrange into a drape (Figure **197**).
4 Repeat the lifting and arranging into folds as shown (Figures **198** and **199**).
5 Trim away the ends and attach to the back of then centre bow at the required angles.

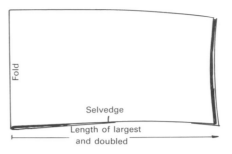

195

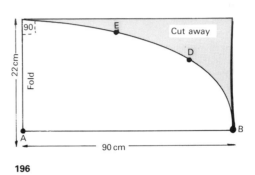

196

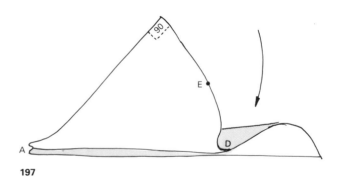

197

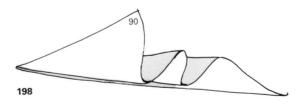

198

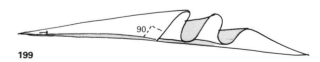

199

FLOWERS

The simple rosette

This roseate can be cut in a firmish fabric like silk taffeta and can be as large or small as the garment design permits.

Method

1 Cut a strip of fabric twice finished width (+ turnings) on the true bias, and angle off both ends (Figure **200**). Sew a large gathering thread along the cut edge.
2 Fold and gather the sewn edge, opening up and twisting until about halfway is reached, then reverse and regather to provide more body to the rosette (Figure **201**).
3 Hand stitch as you go along, winding, feeding and pushing in the gathered fabric.

The snail rose

This rose is based on the circular principle and could be cut in two colours or tones or even two different fabric textures. The finished rose is somewhat flatter than the previous example.

Method

1 Draw a snail shape as the diagram. The size of the snail will depend on the size of the rose required (Figure **202**).
2 Place a gathering thread around the inner edge of the snail (Figure **203**).
3 Open out the snail. Gather and sew as you manipulate the inner edge (Figure **203**).

Figure **204** shows the finished flatter rose. See also plate section.

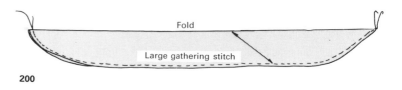

200 Fold / Large gathering stitch

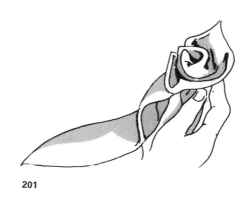

201

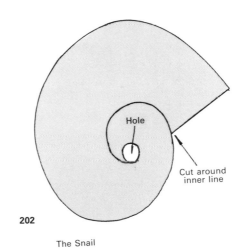

202

Hole

Cut around inner line

The Snail

203 Open out

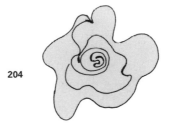

204

VEILS

The wedding dress would not be complete without its veil which adds mystery and romance to the bride's appearance. The choice of the veil's length will depend on factors such as the shape and silhouette of the gown and the headdress which holds the veil in place. The lace and netting for veils can be purchased in various weights, widths and textures and the selected fabric will have a major influence on the size, shape and embellishment of the final veil.

The veil is basically a very simple accessory and can have embellished edges with lace or embroidery or zig-zag stitch or scallops; the list is almost endless. However, all these decorations should be completed when the veil is flat. It is also advisable to round off the corners, as experience has show that the veil is more practical to wear and is less likely to be trodden on by the entourage.

Veils come in three main lengths:

1 The full-length veil which is about 5 m × 3 m.
2 The three-quarter length veil which is about 3 m × 3 m.
3 The shoulder-length veil which is about 2 m × 2 m.

And many variations in between. See plate section.

Method

The full-length veil

1 Cut a length of veiling 5 m × 3 m (Figure **208**).
2 Turn down 1 m as the diagram. Mark off 2 m in the centre of the veil for the top of the head (Figure **209**).
3 Gather this 2 m down to about 10–15 cm depending on the size of the head, and apply to a straight tape to secure. A–B = the top of the head (Figure **210**).
4 Use a comb to secure the veil to the top or back of the head. The headdress can be fixed on to the veil or separately fixed on to a comb.

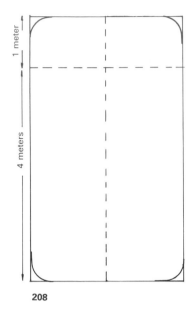

208

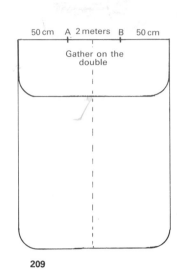

209

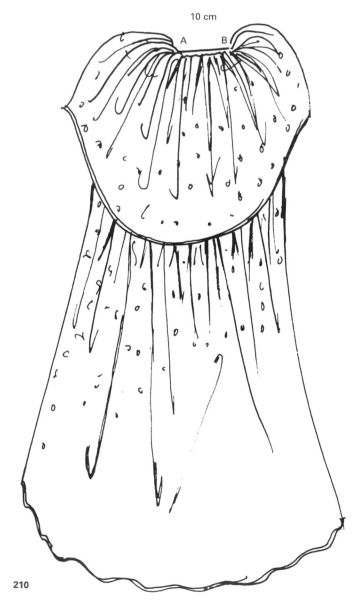

210

The square veil

1 Take a square of a suitable size. Place a diagonal mark from **A** to **B** (Figure **211**).
2 Estimate the amount of turndown to be gathered to the top of the head.
3 Turn down corner **B** and gather to the top of the head as the previous veil (Figure **212**).
4 Secure with a tape of the required size.

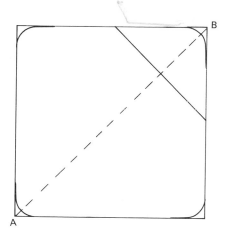

211

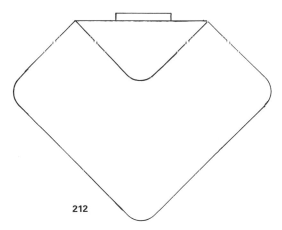

212

Bridal dress 1   The big bow

The back view illustrates the lace appliquéd on to the fabric so that the lace becomes an integral part of the fabric. The ball sleeve with lace fixed to the fabric purely by beads running down the spine of the lace, giving a three-dimensional effect. Also shown is the water fall effect of the train leading into the big bow at the top of the train.

Bridal dress 2
This dress is of crisp paper taffeta. The skirt is cut very slim and overlaid with cowls. The strapless bodice is overlaid with fine piece lace, crystal beaded, and the scalloping outlined with seed pearls. The back train is cut circular with a billowing effect. The very short sleeve is latticed at the crown.

Bridal dress 3   The soufflé
This dress is made of raw silk and is severely cut. The emphasis is on the back soufflé which is held into position by roses made of self-fabric.

Headdresses
A cornet of fresh flowers with the veil just lightly suspended from the back presents a very fresh appearance.

The dramatic effect of the almost overlarge single rose nestling in a cloud of tulle, contrasts the softer effect of three roses of varying size in self-fabric arranged to form a crown supporting a full tulle veil.

Section Three   Basic Skills of Modelling

THE DRESS STAND AND MODELLING THE TOILE

STANDARD PROPORTIONS

In today's industry the dress stand replaces the customer and should be as realistic as is possible in terms of stance, shape and dimensions for the modelling to have any claim to accuracy. Dress stands can be purchased in all industrial sizes, i.e. 10, 12, 14, 16, 18, 20, 22, in women's sizes, and of course men's and children's wear stands can also be purchased. The sample room of a clothing company will have the stock size stand of their particular range. For example the most common size stand in the women's trade is the size 12, but this will vary according to the type of garment manufactured. The following techniques will apply to any size stand.

NON-STANDARD PROPORTIONS

If the garment is intended for a client of non-standard proportions, then it will be necessary to pad out the dress stand in the appropriate areas. For example, for a client with a rather pointed or over-rounded bust, it is often wise to borrow a bra from the client and position it on to the dress stand. Shoulder, pads can be applied to adjust the shoulder slopes; waistlines can be thickened. In other words the basic dress stand can be so developed to take on the contours and stance of the client.

USING THE DRESS TO MODEL THE TOILE

Figure **213** illustrates the dress stand and a 'half toile', the production of which is the objective of this chapter.

There are certain very basic rules or principles which have to be observed when modelling on to the dress stand.

A. Whenever possible apply the fabric to the right-hand side of the body. The right-hand side is often larger than the left, and producing a right-handed toile is a fitting safeguard.
B. Never stretch the fabric on to the figure as this will cause distortions and ruin the subsequent garment. Fabric should be gently but firmly layed on to the dress stand.

General sequence

1 Prepare fabric.
2 Model the front bodice.
3 Model the back bodice.
4 Model the front skirt.
5 Model the back skirt.
6 Mark up the toile.
7 Remove the toile from the stand.
8 Check the accuracy and readjust if necessary.
9 Use the half toile to produce a paper pattern.

Modelling the front bodice

Figures **214** and **215** illustrate the amount of fabric required to model the front bodice.

1 Draw a line 3 cm parallel to the selvedge. The size of the fabric is governed by the height and girth of the body plus handling allowances. This line will fold back and be applied to the centre front (Figure **215**).
2 Mark points **A**−**B**−**C**−**D**−**E** and add allowances as diagram (Figure **215**).
3 Fold line **A**−**C**−**B** (Figure **216**).
4 Apply the folded edge of the fabric to the centre front of the stand (Figure **217**).
5 Use three pins to hold the fabric in place: at the *centre front neck point*, at the *bust line* and at the *waist* (Figure **217**).
6 Place pins every 3 cm to prevent the fabric dragging from the centre front (Figure **217**).
7 Cut off the corner of the fabric at the neck (see the shaded area) and place a pin into the neck point (**G**) (Figure **218**).

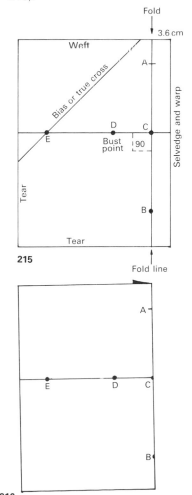

215

216

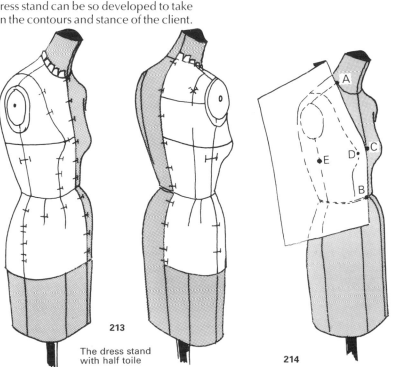

213
The dress stand with half toile

214

8 Using the scissors points, cut down into the neck seam to release the tension around the upper neck (Figure **219**).

The bust suppression

The bust suppression is located above the bust line. To establish the correct amount refer again to Figure **218**.

1 Holding the fabric securely at the *bust point*, raise point **E** until it is horizontal to the floor (Figure **218**).
2 Place a pin into the dress stand to secure the fabric (Figure **218**).
3 The excess amount of fabric which appears between the shoulder point and the neck point is the dart quantity and must be suppressed to create the bust shape (Figure **220**).
4 Bring this amount together and pin down to just above the bust point (Figure **221**).

The waist suppression

1 Use the back of the hand to smooth the fabric down to the waist as the diagram and place a pin into the waist side (Figure **222**).
2 Draw the excess fabric together and a dart will appear from the bust point downwards (Figure **222**).
3 Pin through the fullness to anchor the dart (Figure **222**).
4 To reduce stress and strain at the waistline, cut up to the horizontal folds that will appear at the waist area (Figure **223**).
5 A contoured dart is a dart that closely follows the curves of the bust. Pin the excess amount of fabric closely to the body (Figure **224**).
6 *Note*. If the cloth is under stress at the waist area (see shaded area), remove pins and resmooth the fabric into position (Figure **224**).
7 Figure **225** illustrates the 'stress factor' at the centre front panel due to the non-alignment of the two dart sides. To cure this, slash up the centre of the dart and remodel the centre front stressed side. Figure **226** illustrates the dart slashed open.
8 Reposition the centre front panel so that both sides of the dart lie in harmony with the body (Figure **227**).
9 Repin into position.
10 Note that the front bodice has been divided vertically and horizontally. This clearly illustrates seam positions that will be very useful when developing very fitted garments (Figure **228**).

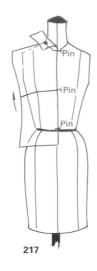

217

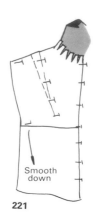

221

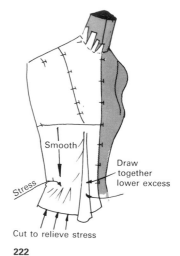

221

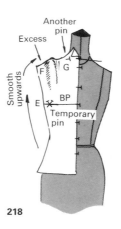

218

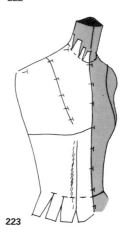

222

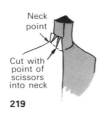

Neck point

Cut with point of scissors into neck

219

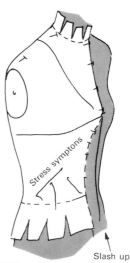

223

220

224

Slash up dart centre

Modelling the back bodice

1 Prepare the fabric as the front bodice (Figures **215** and **216**).

2 The dimensions of the fabric will be the centre back length plus 5 cm either side, by the widest part of the back, i.e. **K–L** at the underarm (Figure **229**).

3 Draw line **H–K–J**, 2.5 cm in from the selvedge (Figure **230**).

4 Draw line **K–L** at 90 degrees from **H–J–K** (Figure **230**).

5 Position the fabric on to the widest part of the back and pin to the centre back as the diagram (Figure **231**).

6 Lift the fabric so that line **K–L** is horizontal to the floor and position a pin at point **M**, which is located at the fullest part of the shoulder (Figure **232**; see also Figure **229**).

7 Place a pin at the shoulder point (**F**) (Figure **233**).

8 Smooth fabric upwards so that the excess fullness appears between point **F** and the neck point. This will be converted into the back shoulder suppression (Figure **233**).

9 The waist suppression should fall from point **N**. Grip this into a dart into the waist (Figure **234**).

10 Figure **235** illustrates the back bodice with the back shoulder dart and the waist dart pinned into position. Slash up to the waist seam to relieve the tension below the waist.

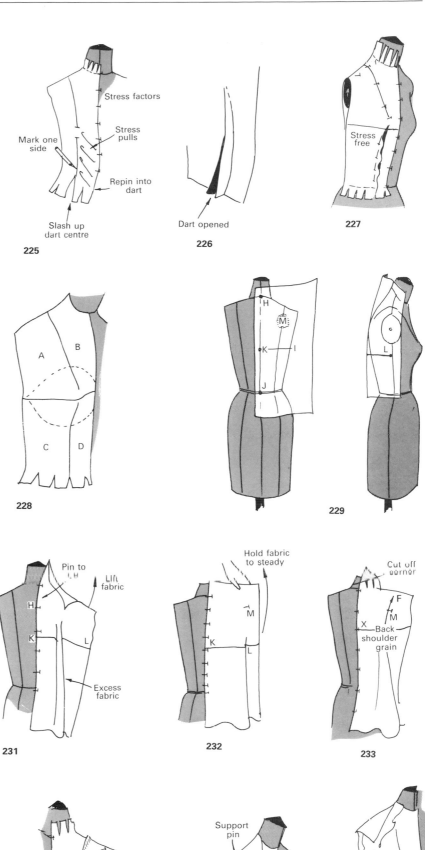

225

226

227

228

229

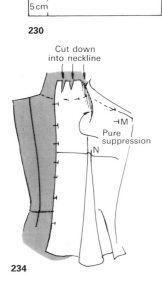

230

231

232

233

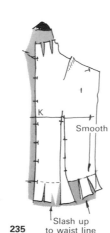

234

235

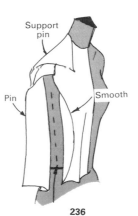

236

237

11 Smooth the fabric downwards from **L** to **O** at the waist and pin into position (Figure **235**).
12 *Note* that both darts converge on to the across back band (Figure **235**).
13 **M** ascertains the half across back width.

The side seams

The next stage is to establish the side seam positions.

1 Expose the side seam of the dress stand (Figure **236**).
2 The front and the back balance are independent of each other therefore unite the front and back side seams at the bust junction with a pin (Figure **237**).
3 Unite the front and back side seams halfway down with a pin (Figure **237**).
4 Unite the side seams from the armhole to the waist with pins.

Joining shoulders

The front and back shoulder balances are different.

1 Unpin the shoulders to reveal the stand underneath (Figure **238**).
2 Feel for the shoulders by gripping the front and back fabrics (Figure **239**).
3 Establish three points: (1) the neck end of shoulder and pin together; (2) mid-shoulder and pin together; (3) end of shoulder and pin together (Figure **239**).

Temporary marking up

The neck ring
1 Feel for the front neck stand seam and using a soft pencil mark through on to the calico (Figure **240**).
2 Feel for the back seam and mark with a soft pencil (Figure **241**).
3 Expose the shoulder (Figure **242**).

4 Lay the back shoulder of the toile on to the stand and overlap the front shoulder on to it using three pins at the major areas (Figure **242**).
5 Check that the neck ring is perfect (Figure **243**).

The side seam and waist ring
The side seam and the waist ring are related.

1 Grip the side seams together allowing tolerance of about 2 cm and place three pins, **A**–**B**–**C**, to hold the fabrics firmly: **A** = pin at the waist; **B** = pin 10 cm up from the waist; **C** = pin 20 cm up from the waist (Figure **244**).
2 Using a pencil mark along line **A**–**B**–**C** (Figure **244**). Point **B** will be used as a balance assembly mark.
3 Trim back seams to 2 cm minimum (Figure **245**).
4 Expose the side seam (Figure **246**).
5 Pin down the front bodice (Figure **247**).

238

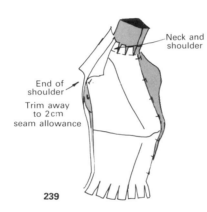

End of shoulder
Trim away to 2 cm seam allowance

Neck and shoulder

239

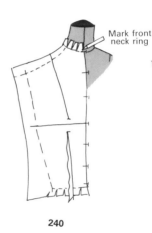

Mark front neck ring

240

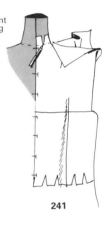

241

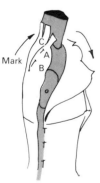

Mark

242

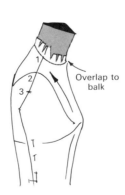

Overlap to balk

243

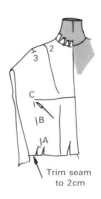

C
B
A

Trim seam to 2 cm

244

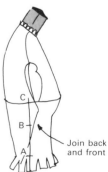

C
B
A

Join back and front

245

6 Fold under the back seam allowance (Figure **247**).

7 Lay the folded edge on to the front seam, carefully matching the three points (see Figures **244** and **245**)

The waist marking sequence
Figures **248** and **249**

(1) Start at the centre back.

(2)/(3) Mark to the dart and place a pin through dart to ensure continuity.

(4) Carry on marking until the side seam is reached and then around to the front dart.

(5)/(6) Pass a pin through the front dart to establish point 6.

(7) Carry on to point 7 at the centre front.

Trim excess away below the waist to about 2 cm.

The armhole ring

There are many armhole depths possible, depending on the degree of movement required in the sleeve. The armhole illustrated here is the *basic fitted armhole*.

1 Locate the hard rim that identifies the shoulder length on the dress stand. Use this landmark to establish the shoulder length (Figure **250**).

2 The minimum sleeveless armhole depth (point **Q**) is approximately 13 cm for a size 12. Measure down from the shoulder end (Figure **251**).

3 Using the Patternmaster square a line at a 90 degree angle from point **Q** (Figure **251**).

4 Draw the scye box, as diagram, to help establish pitch points (Figure **250**).

5 Mark front and back pitch points (Figure **250**).

6 Trim away excess fabric.

The front and back bodices are now complete.

Modelling the skirts

Refer to Figure **213** to see the shape of the front and back skirts. Both skirts have two waist darts. Note that it is only necessary to model them down to the hip line as all skirt lengths are usually extensions of the side seam.

The front skirt

1 Prepare the fabric as previous exercises (Figure **252**).

2 Position the prepared rectangle of fabric on to the front skirt section of the dress stand (Figure **253**).

3 **A**−**B** (at the side seam) add an extra 6 cm (Figure **253**).

4 The 90 degree line **C**−**D** is approximately the hip line (Figure **253**).

246

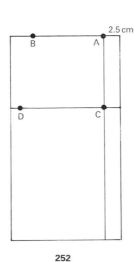

247

248

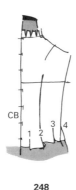

249

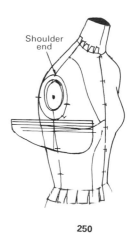

250

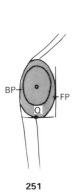

251

252

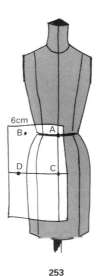

253

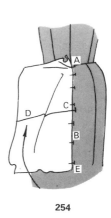

254

5 Place the fabric on to the centre front, folding in the 2.5 cm allowance (Figure **254**).
6 Place a pin at **A**, then **C**, then **E** (Figure **254**).
7 Then position a pin every 3 cm to secure the fabric (Figure **254**).
8 Establish the flat band at the widest part of the trunk which is approximately line **C**–**D**.
9 Place pins **G** and **H** to anchor into position (Figure **255**).
10 Smooth the fabric upwards from **H**: excess fabric will appear at point **A** (Figure **256**).
11 Distribute this excess fabric into two darts, **A** and **B** (Figure **257**).

The back skirt (Figures **258** and **259**)

Use the front modelling sequence to achieve the back skirt.

1 Prepare the fabric.
2 Pin the fabric to the centre back of the stand.
3 Establish the flat band at the widest part of the hip band.
4 Smooth fabric upwards to establish waist suppression.
5 Divide fabric into two amounts.

Marking the side seams

1 Unpin the front and back side seams (Figure **260**).
2 Place a pin at **X** (the widest part of the hip) (Figure **260**).
3 Lay the front skirt on to the stand and mark the waistline (Figure **261**).

4 Mark down to **X** at the hip (Figure **261**).
5 Mark **Y** (halfway between **X** and the waist and **Z** and the waist) (Figure **262**).
6 Mark the waist darts (Figure **262**).
7 Repeat the sequence for the back skirt.

Coupling the side seams

1 Expose the side seams (Figure **262**).
2 Fold the side back seam over the front side seam matching points **X**–**Y**–**Z**, and pin down to the stand (Figure **263**).

At this stage mark up the toile, adding balance marks. Make sure that all seams are marked clearly with pencil. Figure **264** illustrates the marked up toile.

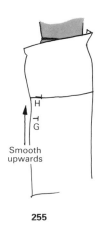

255

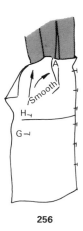

256

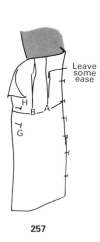

257

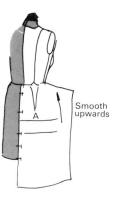

258

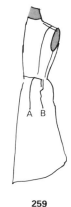

259

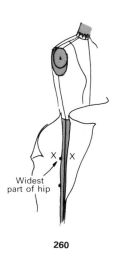

260

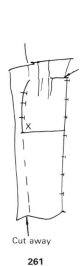

261

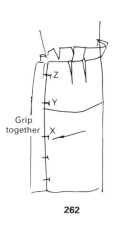

262

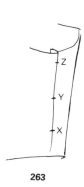

263

The last stage

Flat checking the toile for the skirt is a very important stage. Remove the toile from the stand by unpinning the centre front and the centre back. Before removing the internal pins make sure that all seams are clearly marked.

Correcting the seam runs and curves

The skirts

1 Unpin the skirt and check the accuracy of all back and front balance marks (Figure **264**).
2 Check back and front side seam lengths (Figure **264**).
3 Check that the angle between the back and front skirts at the hem is 90 degrees (Figure **264**).
4 Close out the waist darts and examine the waist run. It should be a clean smooth line from back to front (Figure **265**).

The bodices

1 Unpin the centre front and the centre back and remove the bodice from the stand, *but do not remove the internal pins* (Figure **266**).
2 Check the armhole ring and the side seam as the diagram.
3 Check the waist and side seam runs.
4 Unpin the side seams and check that front and back lengths and runs are the same (Figure **267**).
5 Check the front and back armhole and neck runs (Figure **268**).
6 Remove the shoulder pins and separate the back and front bodices (Figure **269**).
7 Check the dart marking for accuracy before removing pins (Figure **270**).

Figure **271** illustrates the fully marked up front bodice.

8 Completed half basic toile (Figure **272**).

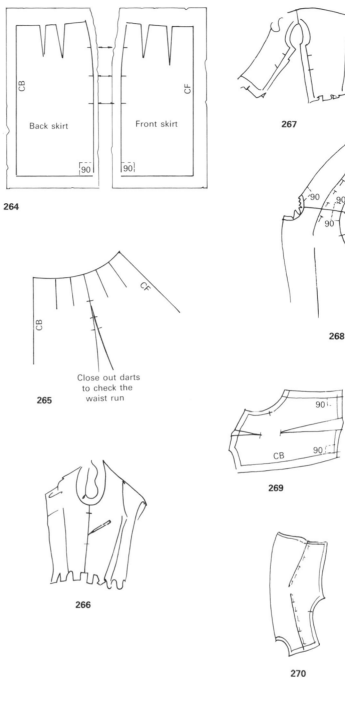

264

265

Close out darts
to check the
waist run

267

268

269

266

270

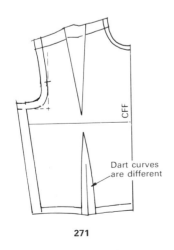

271

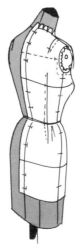

272

Completed half basic toile

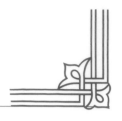

TOILE EVALUATION

What are the specific areas of the toile that need evaluating? The following list will provide firm criteria for those embarking on this course. Whenever possible, use an appropriate-size dress stand and fabric as near to the final fabric as possible. Closely referring to the design (or using the inner creative urges) and selecting the exercise in this book nearest to your design, commence modelling. Continually stand back from the work and adjust line, silhouette, proportion, etc. On completion of the first effort look specifically at the following areas and criteria and pose the following questions.

HAS THE CLOTH BEEN OVER-STRESSED IN THE MODELLING?

Look for the following signs: Does the centre front and the centre back still look straight or has a series of scallops developed down these edges? See Figure **273**. This will probably be caused by the stretching of the fabric in the horizontal plane usually during the formation of the darts.

DOES THE FABRIC LAY SMOOTHLY OVER THE CONTOURS OF THE BODY? IS THE GRAIN BEHAVIOUR TELLING YOU TO ADJUST THE FABRIC?

Look for the following signs: Look carefully at the position of the darts in relation to the contours of the body. Figure **274** shows the effects of poor distribution of suppression and positioning of suppression.

NOW THAT THE SIDE SEAMS HAVE BEEN TURNED IN ARE THEY OPTICALLY STRAIGHT? ARE THEY FULFILLING THEIR PURPOSE IN JOINING THE FRONT AND BACK SECTIONS WITHOUT DISTORTING THE HARMONY AND LAY OF EITHER?

Look for the following signs: In Figure **275**, the side seam back has been shortened and almost dragged down causing the side seam to cockle, it is inclined to pull toward the back. This can be remedied by adjusting the suppressions by lowering the back dart, letting out some of the dart quantity and passing it up to the shoulder dart. In other words unstress the situation.

DOES THE LINE OF THE GARMENT AT SEAM JUNCTIONS FLOW WELL?

Look for the following signs: The shape of the neck, waistline and armhole rings should be continuous, not disjointed and angular, unless of course the design asks for such a shape.

DOES THE SHOULDER SEAM SIT WELL? IS THIS BODY AREA BEING ACCOMMODATED IN LENGTH, SHAPE AND WIDTH?

Look for the following signs: If the shoulder seam does not follow the slight shaping and hollowing that occurs between shoulder and neck point and armhole point, one can detect an area of looseness at the shoulder.

IS THE SHOULDER SEAM LONG ENOUGH FROM NECK POINT TO SHOULDER POINT?

Look for the following sign: The appearance of the garment in this area will take on a pinched look.

HAS SUFFICIENT LENGTH BEEN ALLOWED AT THE BACK ABOVE THE BLADE AREA?

Look for the following sign: If this area is short in length, the balance of the back, especially above the cross back, will cause the back bodice to ride up and distort the balance of the back waistline.

IS THE LOW NECKLINE FITTING CLEANLY WITHOUT GAPING AWAY FROM THE BODY?

Figure **276** illustrates a low cut neckline. In this case it is best to model the bodice to the neck of the stand and then decide what shape the designed neckline should be. Trim the front neckline to within 3 cm of the new neckline. The cloth in this area will tend to be loose. To remedy this, undo the shoulder pins and smooth the front neckline from the centre front upwards and outwards. Repin the shoulder and pivot the extra length through the armhole into the darts. Remark the front shoulder to match the back.

DOES THE FRONT SHOULDER TO BUST DART MEET AND MARRY TO THE DART AT THE BACK SHOULDER?

This is most desirable when producing a toile for a panelled garment. This will affect the fit of the garment and its appearance. Remember that the finished effect is a combination of fit and appearance.

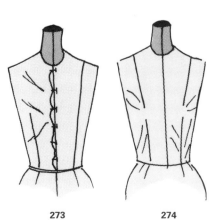

273   274

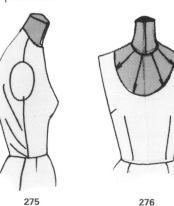

275   276

ARE THERE ANY OTHER AREAS THAT SHOW SIGNS OF STRESS AND STRAIN?

The following exercises and garments will gradually develop the criteria that will aid the examination of the toile for fit and appearance.

THE PRINCIPLES OF DART MANIPULATION

These are illustrated on various bodices and taken through to manipulation on skirts.

PREPARATION

1 Prepare the fabric as for previous bodice examples.
2 Pin the calico down the centre front using pins every 3 cm (Figure **278**).
3 Position bust line at 90 degrees to the centre front (Figure **278**).
4 Using three fingers, as the diagram, smooth across bust line to establish the distance and width between the bust points (Figure **278**).
5 Place anchor pins at: **A**, the shoulder; **B**, the side waist; **C**, the bust line.

The bust suppression and the waist suppression can be repositioned according to the design of the garment without losing fit. To move the bust suppression into the neck as Figure **277**, refer to Figures **279** and **280**.

1 Place fingers under the excess fabric between shoulder and neck point (Figure **279**).
2 Place index finger along the required dart angle at the neck position, lift up the fabric and coax over the centre front so that it lays over the index finger (Figure **279**).
3 Remove the finger from the fold and pin to the stand (Figure **279**).

The waist dart

1 Holding the bust point firmly, coax the lower waist suppression over to the required position at the centre front and pin into position (Figure **280**).

Figure **281** illustrates a bodice with the bust suppression still located above the bust line but positioned into the armhole. Return to Figure **278**.

1 Place pin **A** into the neck (Figure **282**).
2 Place pin **B** at the bust line (Figure **282**).

3 Smooth the bust suppression around to its required position (Figure **282**).
4 Firmly grip the fabric and place pins **A**–**B**–**C** (Figure **283**).
5 Trim the armhole if a finished bodice is required (Figure **283**).

COMBINING TWO DARTS INTO ONE

Figures **284**–**286** illustrate three bodices that have their bust suppression manipulated to below the bust line. The bust suppression can be pivoted into any position and also included into the waist suppression. In fact the total amount of suppression caused by the bust prominence becomes a moveable feast to use as the styles dictate.

277

278

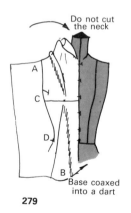

279

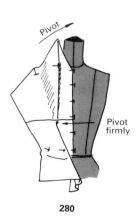

280

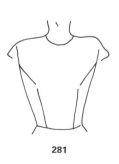

281

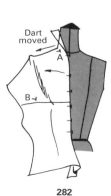

282

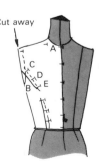

283

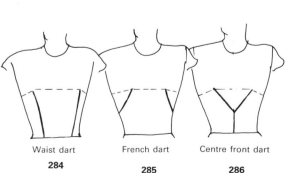

Waist dart
284

French dart
285

Centre front dart
286

The french dart (Figure 285)

Method (Figure 287)

1 Clear the shoulder of darts.
2 Place pin **A** into the neck point and trim away neck excess and release the bust suppression.
3 Using the back of the hand, smooth the excess fabric around to its position just above the bust line.
4 Place pin at **C** to steady the fabric.
5 Place pin at **D** to steady the fabric.
6 Arrange the dart so that it converges on to the bust point and place pins, as diagram, along the dart.
7 Trim away the excess fabric at the side seam and the waist (Figure **288**).
8 Slash up into the waist to clear the horizontal creases (Figure **288**).

The waist dart (Figure 284)

Method (Figure 289)

1 Release the French dart and place a pin at the side waist.
2 The double dart should hang from the bust point, so smooth down the fold from the bust point and pin down as in Figure **290**.
3 Trim the waist and the armhole (Figure **290**).

The centre front dart (Figure 286)

Method

1 Return to Figure **289**. Place finger into the fold at **H** and move the fabric over to its required position at the centre front (Figure **291**).
2 Place a pin at **G** (Figure **292**).
3 To release the waist tension, slash up to the waist (Figure **293**).
4 Mark up the toile as previous exercises.

CREATING FOLDS

Modelling is the ideal medium for developing folds that have a sculptured appearance. The following examples are based on the use of the natural bodice suppression quantities either above or below the bust line.

Folds below the bustline

The two centre folds in Figure **294** are created by using the natural bust suppression which is divided into two sections/amounts.

1 Return to Figure **289**.
2 Smooth down from the armhole to the waist and pin into position (Figure **295**).
3 Slash up to the waist to relieve tension and mark up (Figure **295**).
4 Mark point **L** which is the top of the first fold (Figure **296**).
5 Point **M** is roughly 4 cm, i.e. half the suppression (Figure **296**).
6 Fold the fabric from the bust point so that **M** meets **L**. (Figure **296**).
7 Pin down to secure.
8 Take the remainder of the waist suppression and fold it so that **N** meets the centre front (Figure **297**).

Folds above the bust line

Figures **298** and **299** illustrate two styles in which the entire front suppression is manipulated into folds above the bust line.

Double folds (Figure 298)

Figure **298** illustrates the front bodice with the suppression in the waist area. The objective is to reposition the excess fabric sited below the waist to its new position above the bustline.

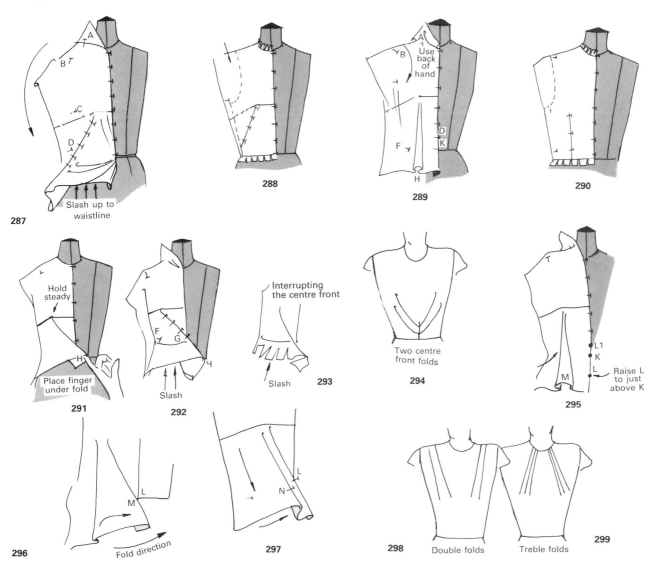

287 Slash up to waistline
288
289
290
291 Hold steady / Place finger under fold
292 Slash
293 Interrupting the centre front / Slash
294 Two centre front folds
295 L1 K L M / Raise L to just above K
296 M L / Fold direction
297 N L
298
299 Double folds   Treble folds

1 Using your spread fingers as a comb, comb and lift the fabric away from the diaphragm (Figure **300**).
2 Place pin **B** to stabilize the fabric.
3 Slash up to the waist line to clear any stress (Figures **301** and **302**).
4 Smooth and comb fabric upwards and pin at shoulder either side of the suppression amount (Figures **303** and **304**). Figure **305** illustrates the total dart quantity.
5 To divide this quantity into two, run the middle finger up the centre of the dart (Figure **305**) and arrange at the shoulder as required by using the fingers as the diagram (Figure **306**).
6 Pin at the shoulder to secure (Figure **307**).

*Treble neck darts (Figure **299**)*

1 Follow on from Figure **304**.
2 Place pin at the shoulder and smooth fabric into the neckline (Figure **308**).
3 Run two fingers up the centre of the dart to divide into three approximately equal amounts (Figure **309**).
4 Place pin at the neck to hold the folds into position (Figure **310**).

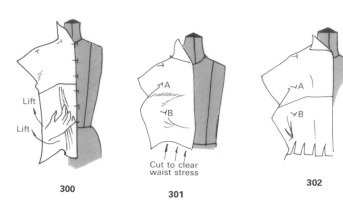

300

301

302

303

304

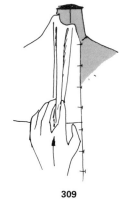

305

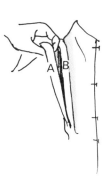

306

307

308

309

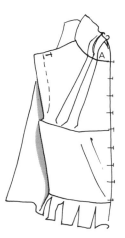

310

FLARED SKIRTS (FIGURE 311)

These diagrams illustrate the method of increasing the hem width of a skirt using the cut and pivot technique.

Preparation

The selvedge of most fabrics is not to be trusted as often it is woven off grain or simply not straight. Therefore bend under 2.5 cm along the selvedge of a rectangle of cloth large enough to cover the front skirt section.

The waist run which will usually finish as a gentle curve. This is achieved by cutting to a given point and placing a control pin, then slashing into the pin and pivoting downwards.

1 Pin the fabric to the dress stand allowing about 6 cm above the waistline (Figure **312**).
2 Decide the point from which the flare will hang.
3 Place anchor pin **A** about one-third in from the centre front (Figure **312**).
4 Cut parallel to the waist then down into pin **A** (Figure **313**).
5 Replace the pin point downwards (Figure **313**).

To float in flare from the upper hip:

1 Wedge open at pin **A** (Figure **314**).
2 Smooth the fabric downwards. The flare should hang from the upper hip (Figure **314**).
3 Repeat for point **B** (Figure **315**).
4 Place pin **B** and cut along the waist and down into the pin (Figure **315**).
5 Replace the pin point downwards.
6 Float the fabric downwards into the hem.

After manipulating the front flare, mark the side seam. If extra flare is required at the side seam from hipline, introduce the extra flare.

1 Decide the flare point.
2 Place pin **C** into the flare point at the side seam (Figure **316**).
3 Cut down the side seam and into the hip (Figure **316**).
4 Replace the pin, point downwards.
5 Float the required amount of fabric into the side seam.

Repeat the centre sequence for the back skirt.

Mark up the waistline and the side seams.

Figure **317** shows the finished shape.

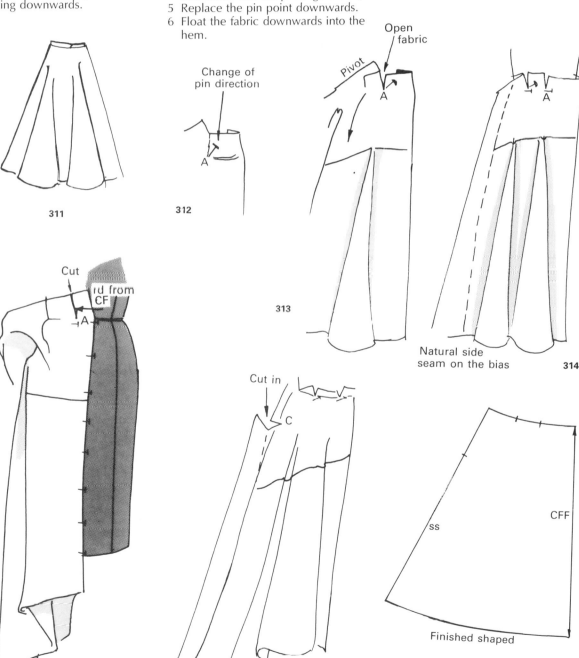

311

312 Change of pin direction

313 Pivot / Open fabric / A

314 Natural side seam on the bias

Cut / rd from CF / A

315

316 Cut in / C

317 ss / CFF / Finished shaped

THE FULL CIRCLE (FIGURE 318)

This full-circle skirt is developed the same way as the gently flared A-line skirt by using the cut and pivot method. The waistline will be divided into at least four sections into which extra flare will be added. Each cut and pivot will add flare to the hem.

1 Pin a large piece of fabric to the dress stand leaving at least 15 cm above the waistline (Figure **319**).
2 Turn in about 3 cm at the selvedge.
3 Place pin **A** at about the quarter of the front waist (Figure **319**).
4 Position the first cut parallel to the front waistline and down into the pin **A** (Figure **319**).
5 Remove the pin and replace the pin point downwards.
6 Pivot the side section downwards to position flare into the skirt (Figure **320**).
7 Repeat this technique along the waistline until the hem has the required amount of flare (Figure **321**).
8 Repeat the sequence for the back skirt.

LEVELLING THE GARMENT HEM

A garment with an uneven hem looks unbalanced and of poor quality. Most garment hems need adjustment at the hemline owing to a number of factors such as the wearer's posture and stance and the fabric stability, i.e. its tendency to drop at certain points due to the grain. Circular skirts have a particular tendency to drop at the cross grain. The general rule is that the fuller the skirt the more cross or bias grain there is and the more the tendency to drop and become uneven. *Note that when a garment is being levelled on a person, the wearer must wear the correct shoes.* The chief objective of levelling is that the hem should be parallel with the floor.

The equipment required is a set square or metre stick, a tape measure and chalk or chalk pencil.

1 Place the garment or toile on to the stand (Figure **322**) or the person.
2 Measure down from the centre back waist to the desired skirt length.
3 Use a set square to measure up from the floor, e.g. **O** to **X**.
4 Keeping the set square static, rotate the dress stand with the skirt applying measurement **O−X** to the fabric marking with chalk or pins every 5 to 10 cm.
5 Cut around the hem allowing a suitable turn up. Note that the width of the hem is crucial and relates to the fullness of the skirt. The fuller the skirt hem the narrower the hem allowance and vice versa.

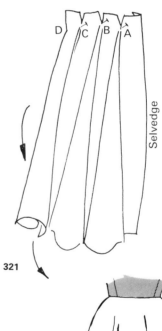

320

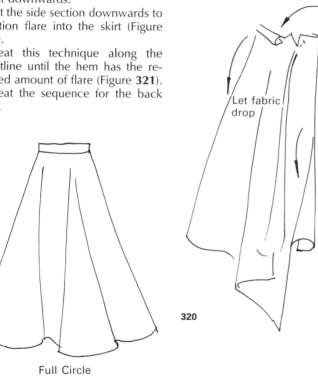

318   Full Circle

321

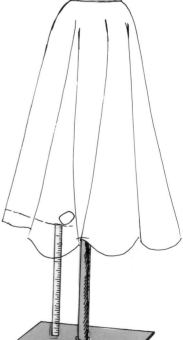

322

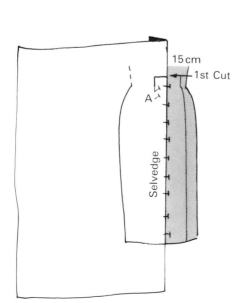

319

BRANDY GLASS AND PEG TOP SHAPES (FIGURE 323)

These following shapes have tapered hems and their fullness is located above the hip area.

1 Prepare the fabric as for previous skirts, bending in 3 cm at the selvedge (Figure **324**).
2 Pin the fabric to the dress stand leaving about 5 cm above the waistline (Figure **324**).
3 Select the narrow area at the base of the dress stand.
4 Hold the fabric square to the dress stand (Figure **324**).
5 Place pin **A** about 3 cm in from the centre front (Figure **324**).

6 Firmly hold point **A** and lift the fabric in the other hand; place pin at **A1** (Figure **325**).
7 Repeat this for **B** and **C**, until the fullness has been located above the hipline and the grain has been lifted (Figure **325**).
8 Pin securely at the side seam (Figure **326**). Note that the fullness above the hipline is more than the natural suppression.
9 Trim away the excess fabric at the side seam to about 3 cm (Figure **327**).
10 Slash into the side seam to help shape the fabric to the stand (Figure **328**).

To convert the fullness into the required folds:

1 Place a finger at the required pleat angle (Figure **329**).
2 Take a quantity of the fabric (i.e. whole amount or division depending on the number of pleats required), bring forward and wrap over the finger to the centre front (Figure **329**).
3 Run finger down the side fold to exit and pin at the top of the fold. Note that wrapping over the finger allows a sculptured effect by inbuilding extra length to the top edge of fold.
4 Repeat this finger wrapping technique until all the excess fullness is used up and the required amount of folds is in position (Figure **330**).
5 If the side seam becomes stressed, remove side seam pins and remodel (Figure **331**).

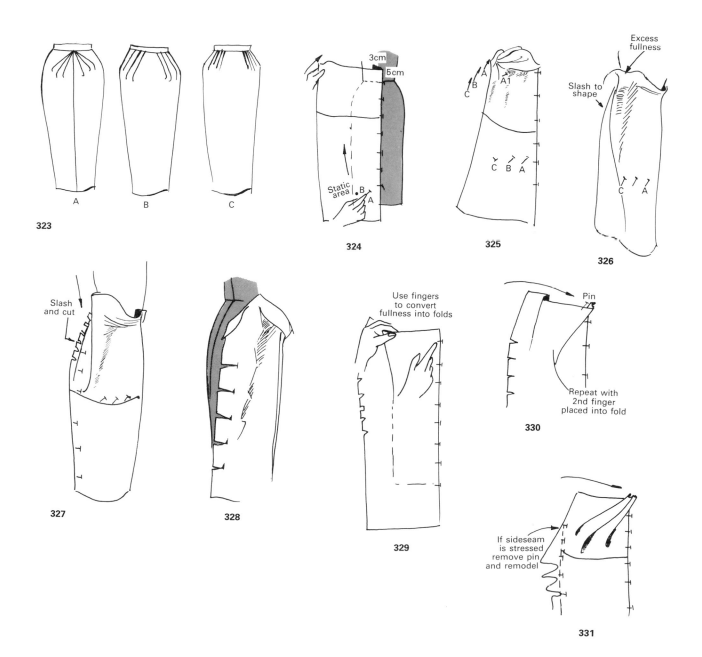

323

324

325

326

327

328

329

330

331

THE WRAP-OVER DRAPE AND WATERFALL (FIGURE 332)

This classical draped skirt is modelled in one piece. It is essential to apply the fabric to the stand so that the straight grain finishes up at the undraped side seam side.

The underskirt

1 Construct a straight skirt with balance marks on to which the draped skirt will be modelled (Figure **333**).
2 Prepare the fabric as the diagram (Figure **334**).
3 Fold down the true bias which will be applied to the waistline (Figure **334**).

4 Apply **A**–**B** (the true bias fold) to the waist. This grain is the most mouldable and will easily smooth around the waistline (Figure **335**).
5 Locate point **D** at approximately the front dart position.
6 Use pins at **A** and **B**.
7 Identify the side seams through the calico.
8 Locate the first drape position at point D and pin.
9 Cut into point **D** to within 3 mm.
10 Lay a hand in the fold direction (Figure **336**).
11 Pick up the required quantity of fabric and raise to point **C**. Leave a finger in the fold and pin over it to establish a longer top edge (Figure **336**).
12 Slide out the finger in the direction of the side seam and place pin **D** (Figure **337**).

13 Place pin **E** at right angles to the side seam (Figure **338**).
14 Cut down the side seam and into pin **E** approximately to within 0.3 cm (Figure **338**).
15 Lift up the fold and pin to the first fold leaving the hand in the fold. Withdraw the hand allowing the fold to have the sculptured look (Figure **339**).
16 Repeat process at **F** for the third fold (Figure **340**).
17 *Note that if the folds miss the pins at the side seam, the fabric is not aligned. To remedy this, adjust by cutting down in towards seam and readjusting (Figure **341**).*
18 Firmly pin the folds together from **A** to **B** (Figure **342**).
19 Cut through all the layers from **A** to **B** to inside bottom fold (Figure **343**).

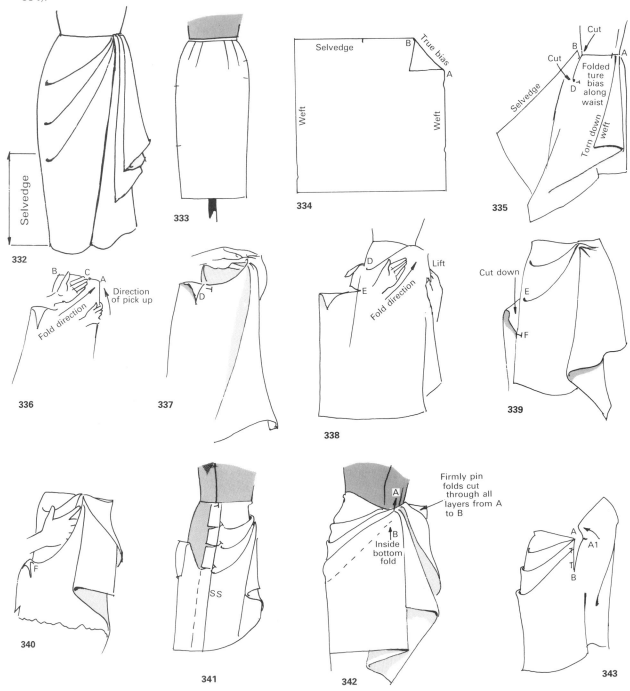

The waterfall

1 Fold over **A1** to **A** (Figure **344**).
2 Arrange the remaining fabric into four folds at **B** (Figure **345**).
3 Locate and mark the waistline at the centre front (Figure **346**).
4 Trim away the fabric above the waistline to release the excess fabric (Figure **347**).
5 Re-examine the folded positions and adjust if required (Figure **348**).
6 Decide the angle of the waterfall by marking points **H−J−K−L** (Figure **348**).
7 Open out the fabric for the waterfall (Figure **349**).
8 Cut from **L** with a smooth curve around through points **K−J−H** (Figure **349**).

Figure **350** illustrates the final waterfalll and drape.

344

345

346

347

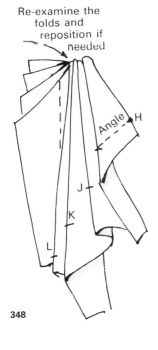

Re-examine the folds and reposition if needed

348

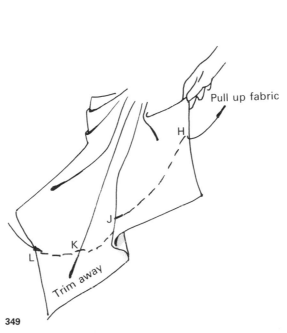

349

350

THE SHEATH DRESS

The main technical feature of this basic-shaped garment is that the waist seam is eliminated, providing the wearer with a very shapely elongated appearance. If this garment is modelled carefully, it will look for all the world as if you have melted the body and poured it into the garment.

THE FRONT

1 Prepare the fabric as previous exercises and fold the selvedge in about 3 cm.
2 Position four pins at the centre front and then fill in every 3 cm (Figure **351**).
3 Smooth the fabric across the bust point to establish the horizontal grain.
4 Manipulate and settle the superfluous fabric between the neck point and the bust point for the bust suppression (Figure **352**).
5 Cut into the neck ring (Figure **353**).
6 Smooth the fabric across the widest part of the hip (Figure **354**).
7 A–B (the centre front length) is the correct body length and it is essential that C–D from the bust to the hip is not tight (Figure **354**).
8 Settle the fabric across the hip; if length C–D is tight, release the bust suppression (which is a moveable feast) into the side seam to increase the side seam contour length (Figure **354**).
9 Gather the vertical waist suppression into one area which could be a false reading of the waist suppression quantity (Figure **354**).
10 To divide or distribute the suppression into a more beneficial position, i.e. one that will more closely assume the contours of the body, run the finger down the centre of dart so that it is divided into two amounts. Pin into position (Figures **355** and **356**).
11 Dart A will satisfy the bust bulge and dart B will accommodate the outer hip bulge (Figure **357**).

Figure **358** shows the finished front.

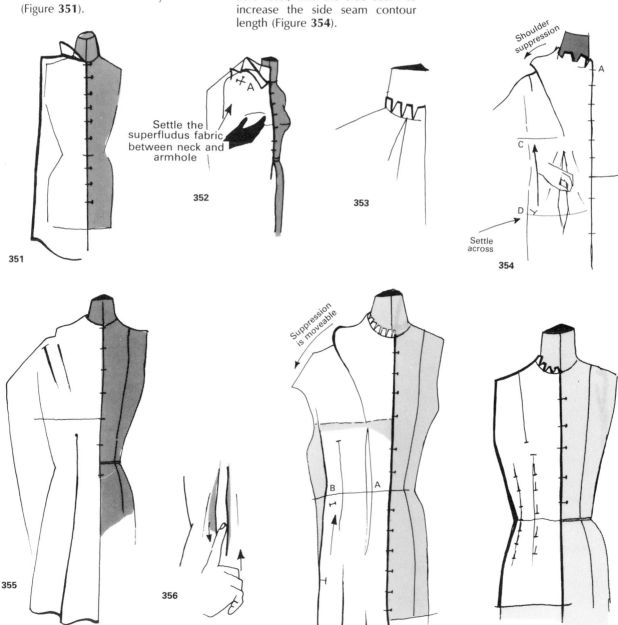

Settle the superfludus fabric between neck and armhole

352

353

Shoulder suppression

Settle across

354

351

355

356

Suppression is moveable

357

358

The back

1. Apply the fabric to the dress stand as previous exercises (Figure **359**).
2. Pin at the shoulder neck point and establish the flat band under the blade suppression by smoothing across the broadest part of the back (Figure **360**).
3. Position the surplus length between the shoulder point and the neck point for the back blade dart (Figure **360**).
4. Place a pin at the side seam at bust level (A) and smooth across the hip area to establish point **B** (Figure **360**).
5. If tightness is felt in the vertical length, release the back blade dart to add extra underarm length.
6. The back dart amount needs disciplining to achieve a good fit and an aesthetic appearance (Figures **361** and **362**).
7. Redistribute the dart two-thirds into the body dart and one-third into the centre back seam as a vertical dart. This vertical suppression takes into account the centre back contour (Figure **362**).

Figure **363** shows the finished back with divided suppression.

Joining the side seams

1. Cut away the excess fabric at the side seam and place balance pins at the underarm point (**A**) the waist (**B**) and the hip (**C**) (Figure **364**).
2. Cut away the excess fabric at the side seams.
3. Pay careful attention to the opposite side, i.e. the front or back. Place pins downwards.

It is important to note that there must be tolerance between the body and the waist and that the garment must not show any stress.

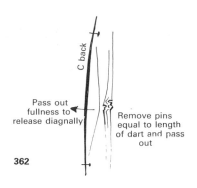

Pass out fullness to release diagnally

C back

Remove pins equal to length of dart and pass out

362

A

B

360

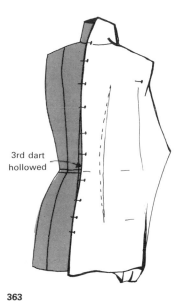

3rd dart hollowed

363

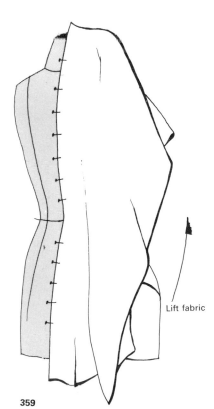

Lift fabric

359

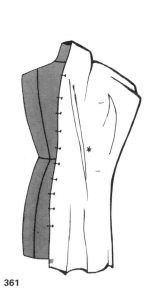

361

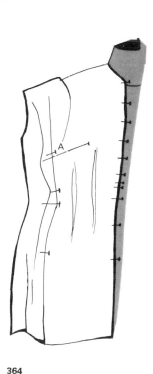

A

364

THE PRINCIPLES OF CIRCLE CUTTING

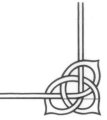

Circular effects from armholes or waist or embellishments such as jabots, frou frous, frills and godets form an essential feature of modelling and can be used with great effect to either decorate or form any garment. Suspended from armholes, necklines, waistlines, hips and other areas, circles have always been an integral part of the fashion silhouette. There are many formulae for cutting circles to an accurate measurement (see page 7). However, modelling is essentially a trial and error experimental medium, and the designer does not always know beforehand what circular proportion is required. The following diagrams illustrate a very simple direct method of cutting a quarter, half or full circle shape without the aid of any calculations.

TO FOLD A QUARTER CIRCLE

1 Take a square of fabric large enough for the intended drape; this will be cut into a quarter circle (Figure **365**).
2 Fold the fabric diagonally (Figure **366**).
3 Repeat the fold four times (Figure **367**).
4 Cut along the base of the folded fabric for the length of the inset (Figures **368** and **369**).
5 Open out the fabric (Figure **370**).

TO FOLD A FULL CIRCLE

1 Cut a square of fabric large enough for the intended drape (Figure **371**).
2 Fold the fabric in half (Figure **372**).
3 Fold the square in half again (Figure **373**).
4 Fold the fabric diagonally (Figure **374**).
5 Fold the corner **EF** to touch the fold and cut away the shaded area (Figure **375**).
6 Open out the fabric and trim around the circular hem (Figure **376**).

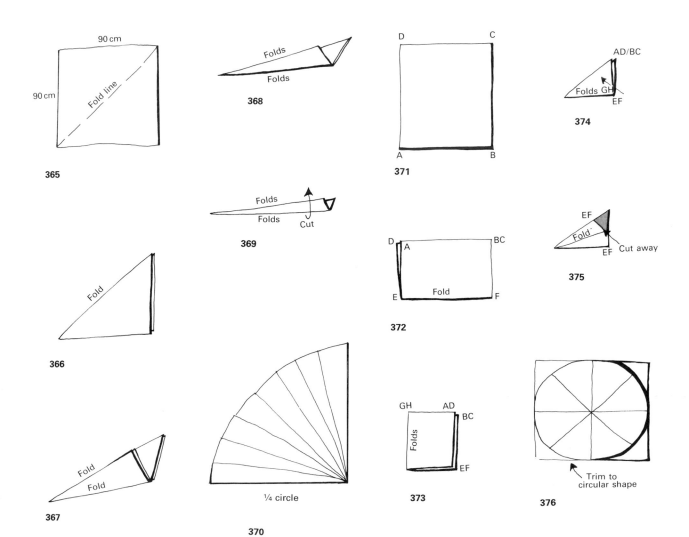

TO FOLD A HALF CIRCLE

1 Cut a rectangle of approximately the correct size (Figure **377**).
2 Fold the fabric in half as the diagram (Figure **378**).
3 Fold again (Figure **379**).
4 Fold again (Figure **380**).
5 Open out the fabric and trim to a half circle (Figure **381**).

377

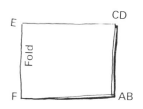

378

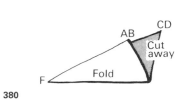

379

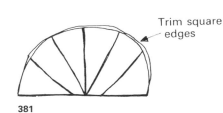

380

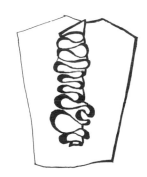

381

382

CIRCULAR EFFECTS

Use single, double or treble ply circles as insets to make some beautiful visual effects.

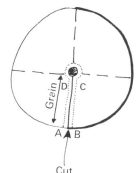

383   Cut

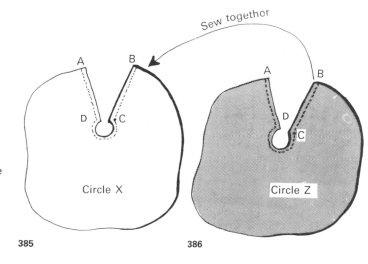

384

385   **386**

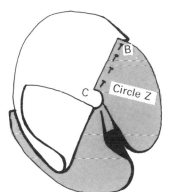

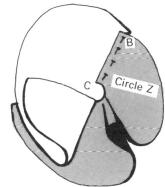

387

Inserted circles into a vertical seam (Figure 382)

Estimate the size of the full circle required and cut three, four or five according to the length of the seam.

Refer to page 72 for method of cutting the full circles. These cicles are then joined together as follows:

1 Cut up the centre of the circle (Figure **383**).
2 A minimum of 0.5 cm is required as a seam (Figure **383**).
3 Cut out a 1 cm hole from the circle centre (Figure **383**).
4 Cut multiples of this circle as many as required, e.g. circle **X** and circle **Z** (Figure **384**).
5 Join circle **X** and **Z** along seamline **A**−**B** (Figures **385** and **386**).
6 Join subsequently to another circle if required which will be labelled C and D and so on. The centre of each circle i.e. **C**−**D**, will be sewn into the vertical seamlines to form the frills (Figure **387**).
7 If the seamlines of the circles are longer than the garment seam, simply ease into the garment seamline, this will give a fuller effect.

Godets

Godets are circular sections that are inset into seams or cut outs and are used for decoration, to add movement and to achieve silhouettes from specified flare points. Godets can be used symmetrically or asymmetrically depending on the effect required. The choice of the godet position will depend on the design and fabric. Godets can be single or multi thickness depending on the weight and stability of the fabric. Godets are more practical when set in as circular cut outs. Figure **388** shows a skirt with flared insets.

1　Model the static or basic skirt shape (Figure **389**).
2　Plan the godet positions (Figure **389**).
3　Distance **A** to **E** should be enough for two 1 cm seams (Figure **389**).
4　Measure **A–B–C–D–E** (Figure **389 (b)**).
5　Cut a half circle (see page 73). **A** to **E** should correspond to **A** to **E** on the skirt (Figure **390**).
6　Inset the godet into the cut line. Use judgement to evaluate the amount of projection required. If the amount is adjudged too great or too small, vary the circle (Figure **391**). Fabric and style are the key factors in this judgement (see Figure **394**).

Figure **392** illustrates the effects obtained by adding circles into flare points at the same level. Figure **393** illustrates godet points at different levels.

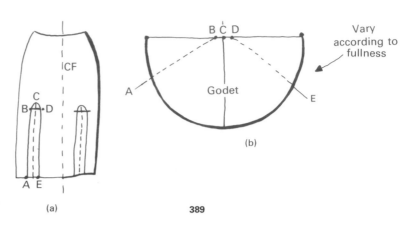

(a)　　　389

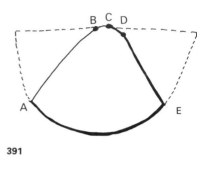

391

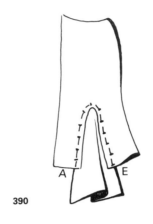

390

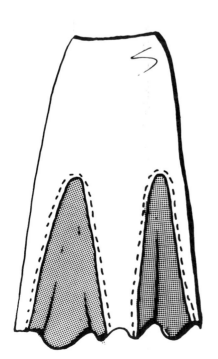

388

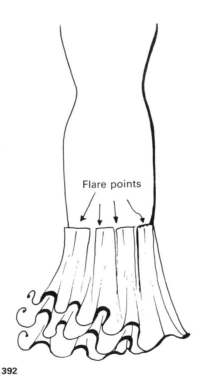

392

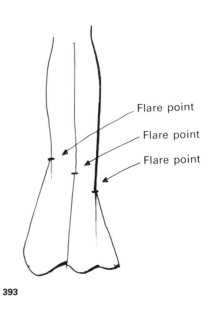

393

1 Model the static silhouette (Figure **394**).
2 Study the silhouette and decide at which points the flare is required (Figure **394**).
3 Use a pencil or style tape to mark the vertical godet lines (Figure **395**).

Godets are more practical when they are circular insets than when they are triangular insets. However, they can be varied according to the weight of the fabric.

Figures **396**, **397** and **398** illustrate the various cuts that can be made.

The chiffon godet (Figure **396**)

A 2 cm seam is taken at the top of the godet and a 1 cm seam at the lower edge. Cut a quarter half or full circle which will inset into the cut **A—B**. The top of the cut is rounded to aid inserting and reduce the pointed corner which often needs reinforcing.

The structured godet (Figure **397**)

This is suitable for a very firm fabric. The point is reinforced.

Figures **397** and **398** illustrate two types of 'cuts' into which the godet can be inserted.

Figures **399** and **400** illustrate a godet of three or four thicknesses, cut as circles of varying lengths and inset into the cut.

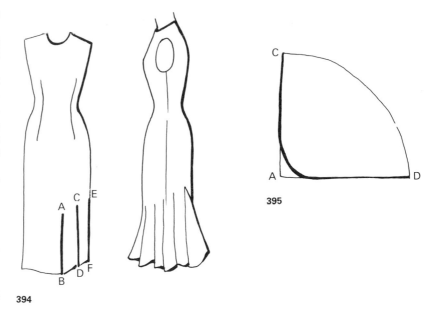

394

395

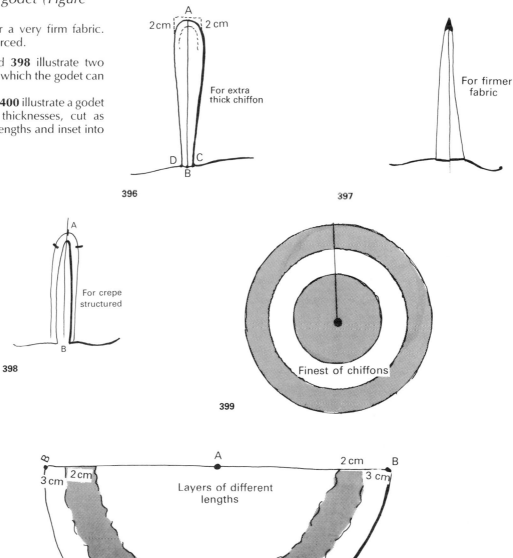

396

397

398

399

400

SLEEVES

This chapter is all about the modelling and cutting of sleeves. It progresses from simple basic sleeves to some very complicated unusual bias-cut and draped sleeves which are highly influenced by the draping skills found in the 1930s. It is essential to have a padded arm on which to drape these styles as most of the sleeves are developed away from the dress stand.

THE PADDED ARM (SIZE 12) (FIGURE 405)

Figure **405** is divided into 2 cm grids. Trace off each section. Note that seam allowances are not included. Sew each section together and pad out with cotton wool or a similar padding.

STRAIGHT SLEEVE WITH ELBOW DART

1 Take a length of fabric at least 10 cm larger than the width of the arm (Figure **401**).
2 Lay the arm on to the fabric (which is folded) to ascertain the length and width required (Figure **402**).
3 Fold the crown to biceps line down and crease lightly (Figure **402**).
4 Open out the fabric and mark the vertical and horizontal lines with a pencil (Figure **403**).
5 The line on the arm is curved; the straight line **A–B** will now appear to be curved and run from the centre sleeve head straight down to the elbow and onwards to the little finger position. The dotted line marks the limb centre (Figure **404**).

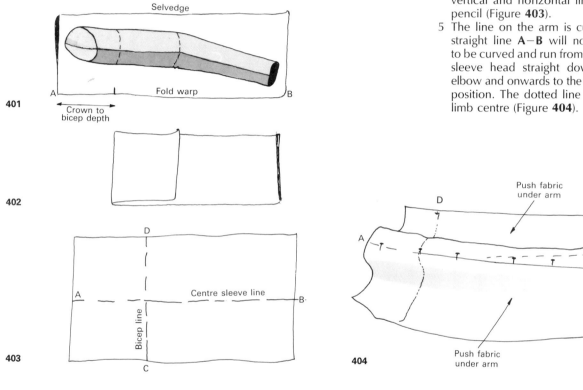

401 Selvedge / Fold warp / A / B / Crown to bicep depth

402

403 D / A / Centre sleeve line / B / Bicep line / C

404 D / A / B / Push fabric under arm / Push fabric under arm

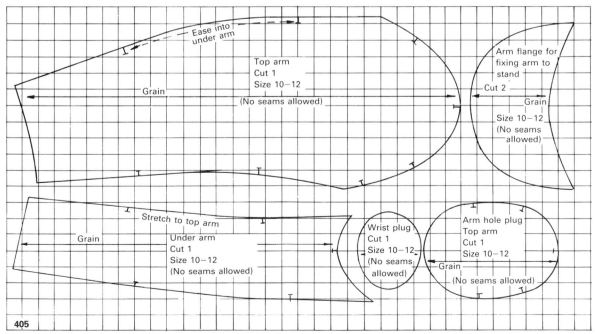

405 Ease into under arm / Top arm Cut 1 Size 10–12 (No seams allowed) / Grain / Arm flange for fixing arm to stand Cut 2 Grain Size 10–12 (No seams allowed) / Stretch to top arm / Under arm Cut 1 Size 10–12 (No seams allowed) / Grain / Wrist plug Cut 1 Size 10–12 (No seams allowed) / Arm hole plug Top arm Cut 1 Size 10–12 Grain (No seams allowed)

The wrapping around stage (Figure 406)

1 Gently coax the fabric under the arm until the line **C**−**D** meets. The curve of the limb will allow a dart to formulate.
2 Pin a dart from the elbow point to the wrist. The quantity in the dart depends on the curve of the limb. *Do not model too closely to the arm. Tolerance must be allowed.*
3 Join together points **C** and **D** (Figure 407). Note that the line pinned from the front pitch to the thumb position is a straight line.

Figure **408** shows the tube wrapped around the arm and the elbow dart.

The sleeve head

1 Measure 13 cm up from point **E** for the sleeve head. Place a pin for point **F**. Trim away the excess fabric as in Figure **407** (Figure **409**).
2 Remove the arm from the sleeve (Figure **410**).
3 Pick up points **C**−**D** (Figure **410**).

Close in the sleeve

1 Match up the underarm balance marks so that the seam allowances are enclosed (Figure **411**).

The sleeve hang

The sleeve hang or pitch is determined by eye.

1 Relate the straight line **A**−**B** on the sleeve to the side seam at **B**. If parallel, the sleeve is pleasantly angled foreward. Pin the crown to the shoulder (Figure **412**).

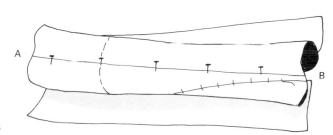

406

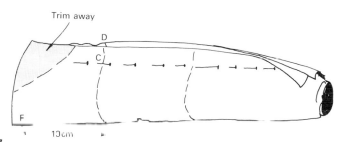

407

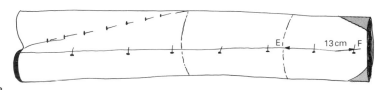

408

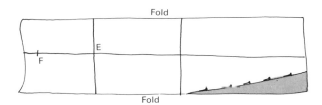

409

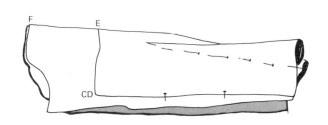

410

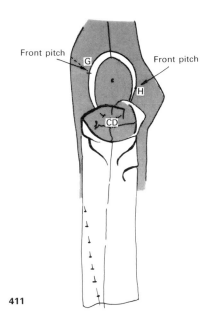

411

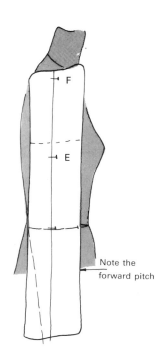

412

The armhole and sleeve head

1 Temporarily anchor the sleeve to the bodice to relieve both hands (Figure **413**).
2 Continue pinning inside the sleeve up to **H** on the front and up to **G** at the back armhole, thereby creating from the armhole the area of the sleeve head. Allow a little ease around these curves (Figure **414**).
3 Cut into **F** and **B** and pitch **G**–**H** to overlay the excess fabric over the front bodice armhole. Be prepared to elongate the crown height **E**–**F** if necessary (Figure **414**).
4 Ease in fabric from **H** to **G** for the crown ease. Trace through the sleeve crown run to the armhole and place balance marks as the diagram (Figure **414**).
5 Trim away around the crown and remove the sleeve from the stand and open the fabric out (Figure **415**).

Check points

The sleeve must not show any tension at the scye base. Mark the underarm of the sleeve by tracing through from the base of the bodice.

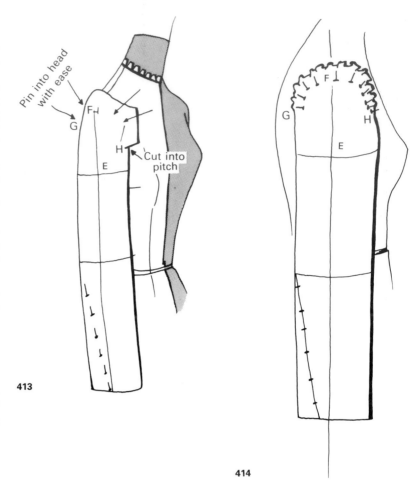

413

414

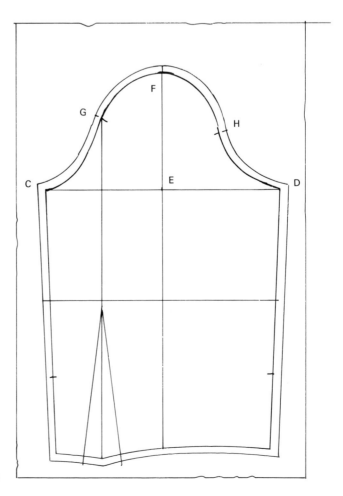

415

BIAS TIGHT FITTING SLEEVE (FIGURE 416)

This sleeve is often used in wedding dresses. The fabric selected should be spongy rather than closely woven, i.e. moss crepe, soft and fine wool, etc.

1 Strike off a square of fabric and test it for length and width by laying the arm on to it. Finger crease the true bias and open out the fabric (Figure **418**).
2 Lay the true bias down the centre line of the arm (Figure **418**).
3 Mark up the fabric (Figure **417**).
4 Lay the fabric over the padded arm and coax the fabric to cover the limb following the contours of the arm with the straight true bias line (Figure **419**).
5 Model closer to the arm than the previous sleeve (Figure **420**).
6 Roll the sleeve on to its back and pin the underarm (Figure **420**).
7 Lay the top of the sleeve downwards on the table and concentrate the suppression at the crook of the elbow (the inside), then disperse this suppression (Figure **420**). (Figure **420**).
8 Ease the front underarm seam into the back, i.e. into a space 7 cm above and below the crook of the elbow (Figure **420**).
9 The crown is achieved as before, but the crown height may not be high due to the true bias being used (Figure **420**).
10 Trim away the excess fullness on the crown and mark the underarm seam. Note that in the bias sleeve the area of easing over the crown is slightly fuller (Figure **420**).
11 Place a balance mark on the underarm sleeve seam (Figure **420**).

Figure **421** shows the finished sleeve with corrected lines. Refer to the previous style for the armhole position. Note: there is no need for a wrist–elbow dart in a bias cut sleeve.

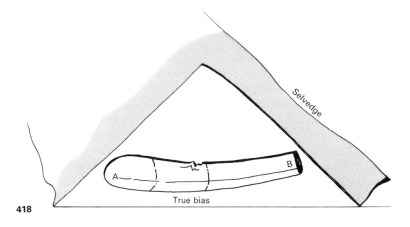

418

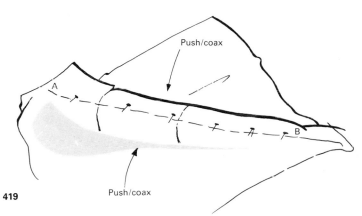

419

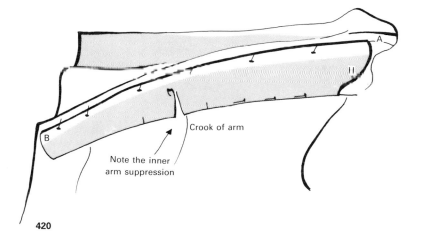

420

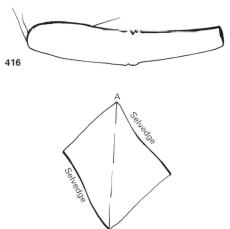

416

417

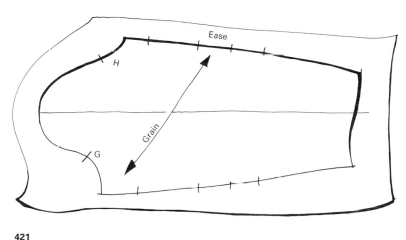

421

COWL SLEEVES (FIGURES 422–424)

The following draped sleeves are based on the cowl principle and are a variation of the same sleeve.

1 Fold a large square of fabric the dimensions of which are approximately the length of the arm (Figure **425**).
2 Position the arm on to the folded fabric (Figure **425**).
3 The distance from **C**–**B** shall equal the amount of projection required (Figure **425**).
4 Trim away the shaded sections of fabric and pin along the seam lines and turn in the seam (Figure **425 (a)**).
5 Open up the fabric and place the arm into the fabric, following the underarm position; pin the undersleeve which is on the bias to it (Figure **425 (b)**).
6 Establish point **X** and poke it in to achieve the cowl look and anchor (Figure **426**).
7 A double cowl can be achieved if required. If the fabric does not sit inside the cowl it will need to be trimmed away to remove the excess length (Figure **427**).

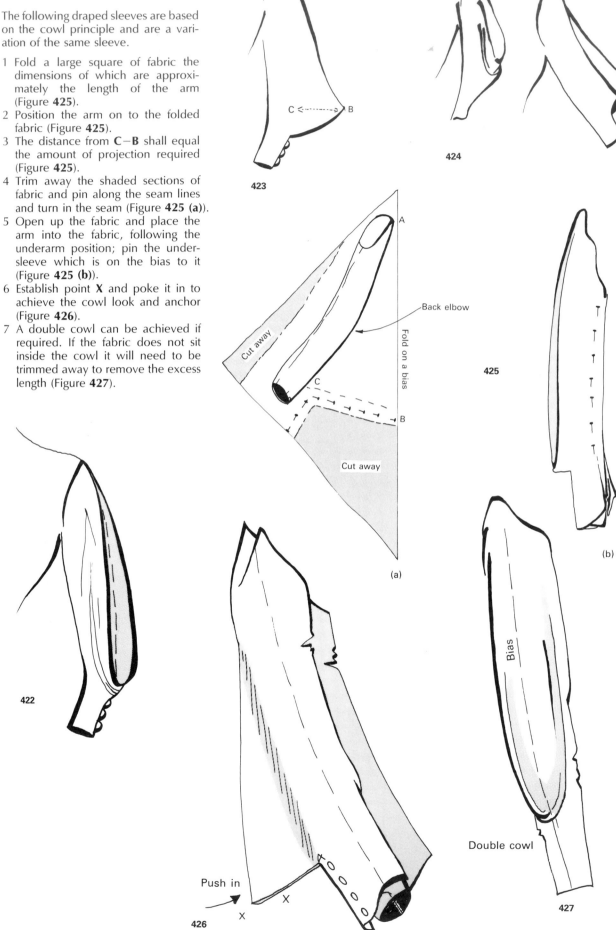

The sleeve head (Figure 428)

For the sleeve head use the basic flat sleeve block. Before removing the toile mark the crown and underarm points. These will be used as a guide, or cut the sleeve in paper plus 5 cm of underarm.

THE NATURAL COWL SLEEVE (FIGURE 429)

The fabric choice depends on the required effect. For a very sculptured effect a tighter weave is required. A flowing sleeve which appears to be a casual happening needs a crepe or jersey fabric.

To start this sleeve, position the paper crown on to the stuffed limb prior to starting.

1 Gauge the dimensions of the fabric by laying the sleeve on to the folded fabric (Figure **431**).
2 Open up the fabric and estimate the distance or depth from the crown to the front drape, e.g. **A–B** (Figure **432**).
3 Mark through on the fabric points **A–B–A** (Figure **432**).
4 Trim away the corner (Figure **432**).
5 Fold the fabric (Figure **433**).
6 Hang the limb and place the fabric on to the arm points **A** meeting at the centre crown (Figure **434**).
7 Fold the fabric downwards to achieve the cowls (Figure **435**).
8 Pick up the fabric on the bias for the next cowl and lift at the crown (Figure **435**).
9 If the top fold is too high, recompose the amount showing by folding more fabric under (Figure **436**).
10 Trim away the excess fabric at the underarm and sleeve head. Tidy up the crown (Figure **436**).

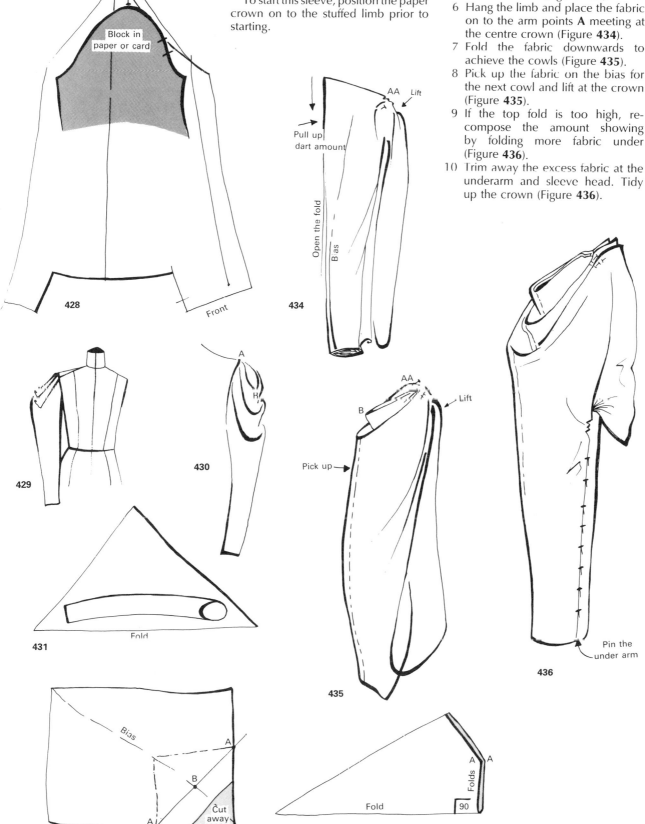

428

429

430

431

434

435

436

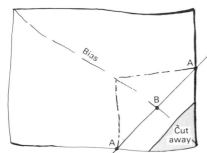

432

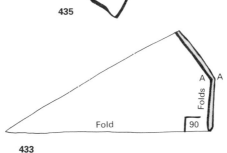

433

THE BALL SLEEVE

This sleeve was used a great deal in Victorian times. This version is cut from a circle of cloth and can be used in three ways:

1 Set into an extended shoulder (Figure **437**).
2 Set into a normal armhole (Figure **438**).
3 Cut and set into a lower armhole and elasticated (Figure **439**).

The thickness of the fabric will dictate the size of the circle, i.e. the volume needed. If organza is used, a larger square will be needed because of the fabric weight.

1 Cut a square the correct size depending on the above factors (Figure **440**).
2 Cut a circle by the process described in previous chapters (Figure **441**).
3 Fold the circle on the bias (Figure **442**).
4 Position the fabric or to the arm allowing as much ballooning as required (Figure **443**).
5 Looking at the sketch, calculate the underarm length, e.g. **C**–**B**; **A** = shoulder, **B** = round upperarm, **C** = underarm, **D** = underarm point (Figure **444**).
6 Cut a circle from **B** to **C** as the diagram and and nip into **B** and **C** (Figure **445**).
7 Push the arm through the hole (Figure **446**).
8 Turn over the arm and affix to the dress stand (Figure **447**).

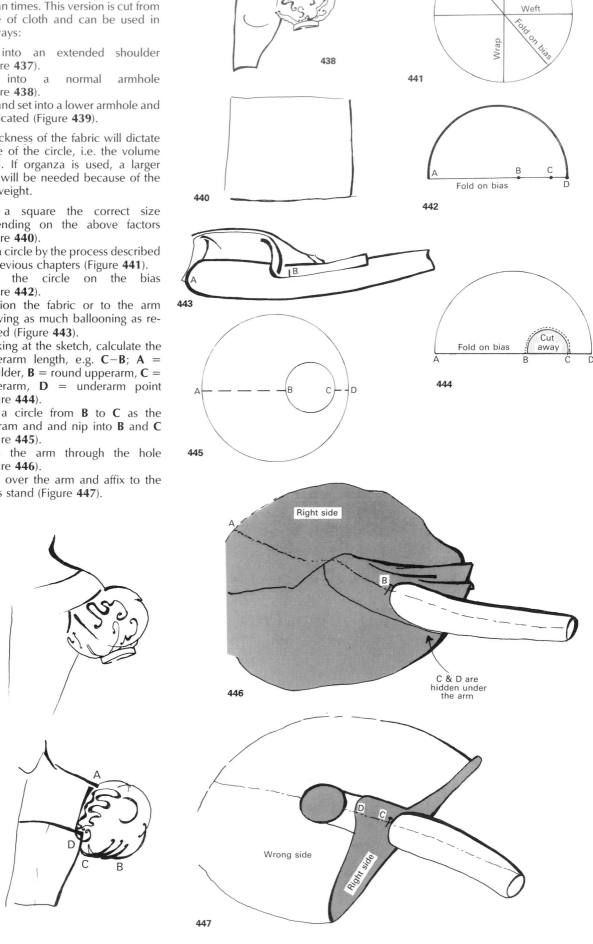

The gathering

1. Place a gathering thread around the circle and hold up the arm or suspend the arm from the stand and gather the circle to the arm (Figure **448**).
2. If there is too much fabric, judgement must be used to decide if the volume of the circle is too large. Figure **449** is the sleeve viewed from the top.
3. If the volume is too great, remove the outer circumference by using squat darts. The dart quantities are approximately 4 cm × 4 cm in length. This will reduce about half the excess circumference (Figure **450**).
4. Sew the darts, trim away leaving 0.8 cm turning, press open and gather the rest.
5. If gathering is required at the upper arm, trim away a larger hole.

THE LATTICE SLEEVE (FIGURE 451)

This complex sleeve is modelled on to a padded arm and also requires a flat sleeve in lining.

Prepare the arm and armhole.

The surface

1. Find the optical centre of the sleeve and draw a line. Pin a narrow tape on to the sleeve centre line (Figure **452**).
2. The fabric length should be approximately one and a half times the length of the limb at least 91 cm width. Fold lengthwise on straight grain. Finger press (Figure **453**).
3. Evaluate the limb and focus in on the first crossover point Place crossover pins according to the style (Figure **453**).

4. Finger fold the fabric (Figure **453**).
5. Apply the fabric to the arm so that **A**−**B** on the fabric is about one and a half times **A**−**B** on the arm (Figure **454**).
6. Apply to the arm to match **A**−**A**.
7. Pin **B** to **B** so that the fabric pouches at the crown.
8. Point **C** from **A** is about 4 cm on the diagonal. Pick up point **C** and overlap (Figure **455**).
9. Place a pin into **D** (the second crossover point) (Figure **455**).
10. Pick up **E** and fold over to **D** (Figure **456**).
11. Carry on picking up and folding over until all folds are accomplished (Figure **457**).
12. Mark the centre line with a pencil and mark along 4 cm on each fold, as the diagram, and also along the wrist (Figure **457**).
13. Place pins to hold the folds in place (Figure **457**).

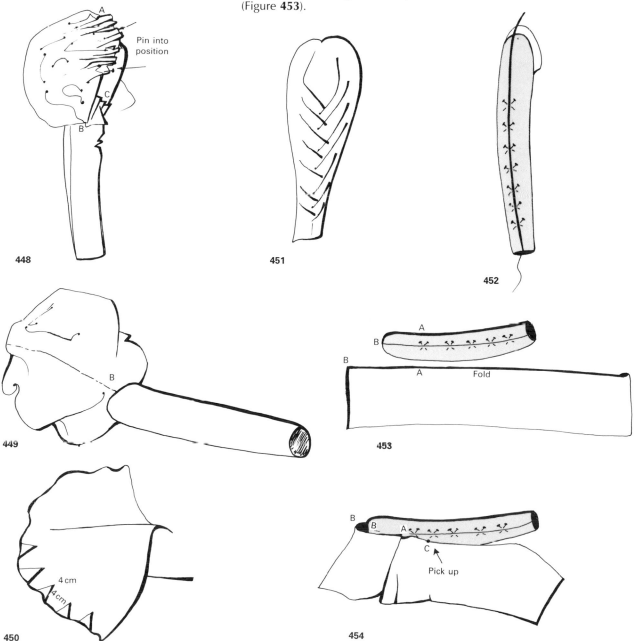

448

449

450

451

452

453

454

The hidden element

Turn over the arm.

1 Coax the fabric around and afix to the underarm and find the approximate underarm position (Figure **458**).
2 Place pins to hold into position and draw the underarm line (Figure **458**).
3 Trim away the unnecessary fabric.
4 Pleat over the crown to make head fullness (Figure **459**).
5 Trim away underarm surplus.
6 Make a provisional mark on the top arm itself for the first crossover with pencil or a tack (Figure **460**).
7 Remove all pins having checked that all folds have been marked (Figure **460**).
8 Place three balance marks on the underarm **G**–**H**–**J** (Figure **460**).
9 Remove the toile from the arm removing all the pins; trace wheel through all the solid boxes, pleat

lines and end caps, mark with a pencil (Figure **460**).
10 Turn over and repeat marking on the underside (Figure **460**).
11 Cut up the dotted lines approximately half way between black lines (Figure **460**).
12 Open up the double sleeve (Figure **461**).
13 Cut up the centre to the first cut **C** (Figure **461**).
14 Lay the open fabric on to the arm (Figure **462**).
15 Pin at point **A** (Figure **462**).
16 Pick up the first box (Figure **463**). Right- and left-hand latticing. Note: Reverse for left sleeve to achieve the pair.
17 Ensure that the centre line carries on through lines indicated on the arm (Figure **463**).
18 Pick up **D** on the angled line and position over **E** (Figure **463**).
19 Pin down at the centre and 4 cm points (Figure **464**).
20 Pick up **D** on the back and lattice

over **D** (Figure **464**).
21 Carry on picking up and positioning over to reach the wrist. Adjust the unequal lengths if necessary by re-adjusting the folds (Figure **464**).
22 After pleating the sleeve, turn the sleeve over and match the underarm sleeve balance (Figure **465**).
23 The underarm will probably need adjusting. The front underarm may need repinning to the back underarm (Figure **466**).
24 Cut away unnecessary fabric from the underarm.
25 Place a gathering thread along the sleeve head and gather and pin to the sleeve crown 12 cm either side of the centre line; arrange the sleeve head as required (Figure **466**).
26 Cut away surplus fabric for the armhole (Figure **467**).

This sleeve must be mounted on to a fitted lining. Figure **468** shows the finished sleeve side view.

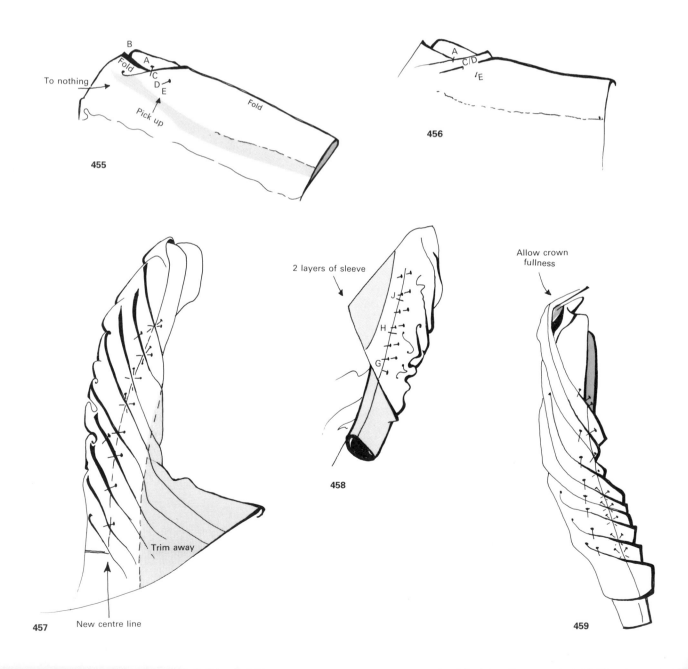

455

456

457   New centre line

458

459

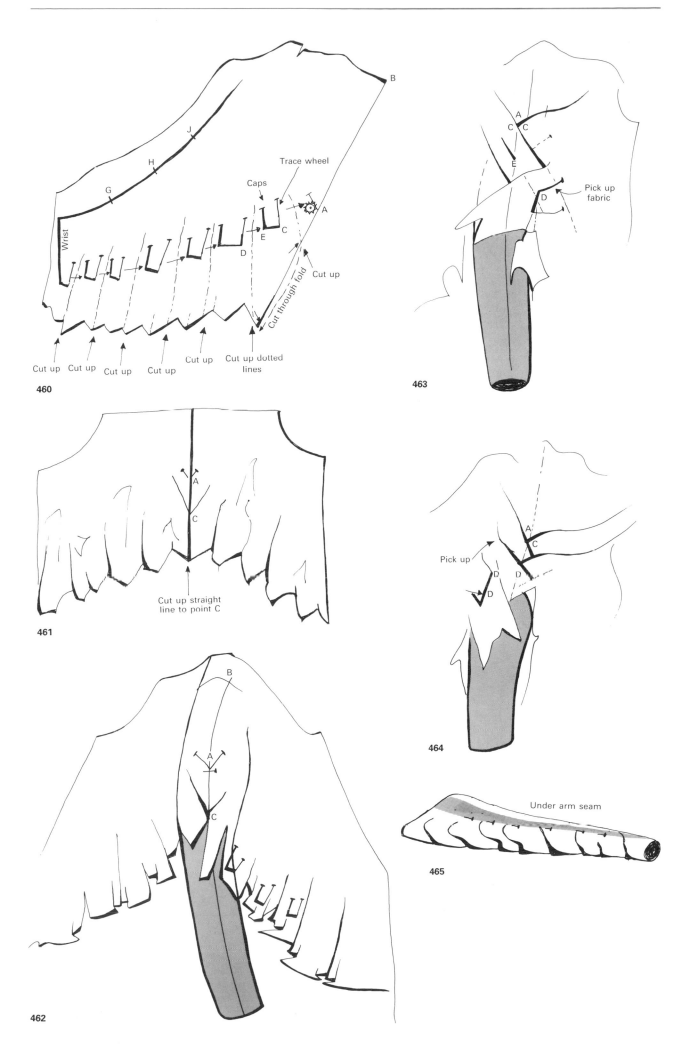

460

Trace wheel

Caps

A

C

E

D

Wrist

Cut through fold

Cut up

Cut up   Cut up   Cut up   Cut up   Cut up   Cut up dotted
lines

B

J

H

G

461

A

C

Cut up straight
line to point C

462

B

A

C

463

A

C   C

E

D

Pick up
fabric

464

Pick up

A

C

D   D

D

465

Under arm seam

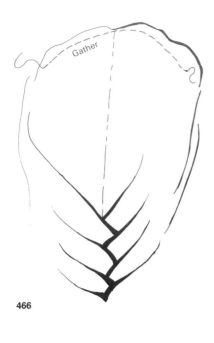

466

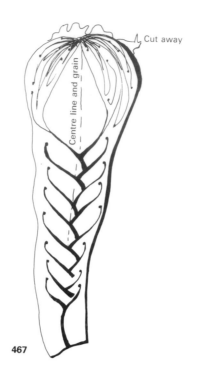

467

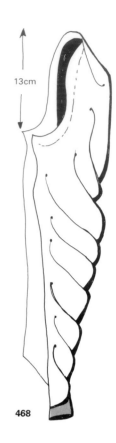

13cm

Cut away

468

THE DOLMAN SLEEVE AND VARIATIONS (FIGURES 469–471)

The fabric for this sleeve must be fluid, ideally a silk jersey or a fine wool crepe.

1 Halve a large square of fabric diagonally. Finger press along the bias (Figure **472** and **473**).
2 Open out the fabric and pencil mark the true bias (Figure **473**).
3 Place the padded arm on to the stand (Figure **474**).
4 Place the fabric on to the hip of the stand as the diagram. Cut away the folded back point leaving a 3 cm turning (Figure **475**).
5 Cut down into the waist (Figure **476**).
6 Pull the back fabric upwards on to the suspended arm (Figure **477**).
7 Trim away the excess fabric above the arm; test the sleeve for drape (Figure **478**).

Coupling up back and front

1 With the arm down in repose follow the arm centre line which will be curved to the front (Figure **479**).
2 Make sure that when joining the sleeve the modelling is loose (Figure **480**).
3 Remove the sleeve from the stand and position balance marks down the sleeve seam (Figure **481**).

Figure **481** shows the finished shape.

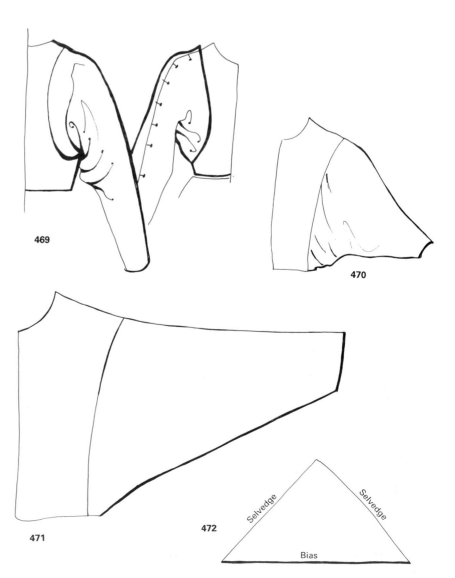

469

470

471

472

Selvedge   Selvedge

Bias

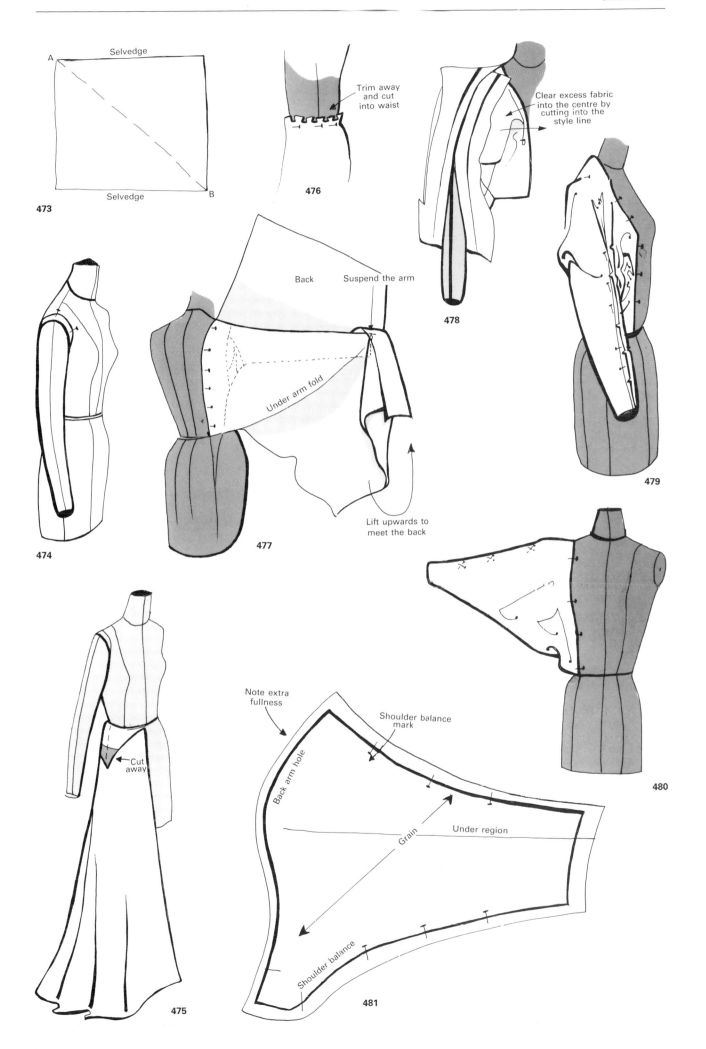

473

Selvedge

A

Selvedge

B

476

Trim away
and cut
into waist

Clear excess fabric
into the centre by
cutting into the
style line

478

479

474

Back

Suspend the arm

Under arm fold

Lift upwards to
meet the back

477

480

475

Cut
away

Note extra
fullness

Shoulder balance
mark

Back arm hole

Grain

Under region

Shoulder balance

481

COLLARS

Collars come in two basic shapes, the standing up variety (Figure **482**) and the laying down variety (Figure **483**). Between these two broad categories there are a countless number of variations. What follows are the collar modelling techniques which demonstrate the basic collars and will provide a framework on which to develop many interesting collar styles.

THE STAND OR MANDARIN COLLAR

The stand or mandarin collar is a starting point for a variety of collar styles. The height limitation is based on the neck height, and, after experimentation, wider widths can be used.

1 Model the bodice according to your chosen design and mark out the neckline from the actual stand seams (Figure **484**).

2 Scoop out a neckline lowering the centre front by 0.5 cm to 0.7 cm to afford comfort to the wearer (Figure **485**).
3 Fabric required is about four times the finished width for the height. Cut rectangle as diagram (Figure **486**).
4 Apply the rectangle to the back neck (Figure **487**).
5 Cut through to point **B** about 4 cm in from the centre back, up to the base of the neck (Figure **487**). The objective is to manipulate the top fabric edge around the neck.
6 Feel around the neck ring and continue to cut up to it (Figure **488**).
7 Finally cut up to the centre front (Figure **489**).

Figure **490** shows the mandarin collar.

Figures **491**–**493** illustrate a stand collar ending in a wing turnback. Trace through the neck ring and collar ring so that they merge exactly.

PETER PAN COLLAR

This collar commences with the fabric facing downwards.

1 The fabric requirements for this collar is about two and a half times the collar finished width (Figure **494**).
2 Cut in above the neck and then down into the neck circle (Figure **495**).
3 Mark in the back neck circle and balance mark at the shoulder (Figure **495**).
4 Continue cutting down into the neck (Figure **496**).
5 Figure **497** illustrates the collar continued to the centre front. Place balance marks at the shoulder and half way to the centre front.

Figure **497** shows the Peter Pan collar shape and also a variation. Figure **498** shows the finished shape.

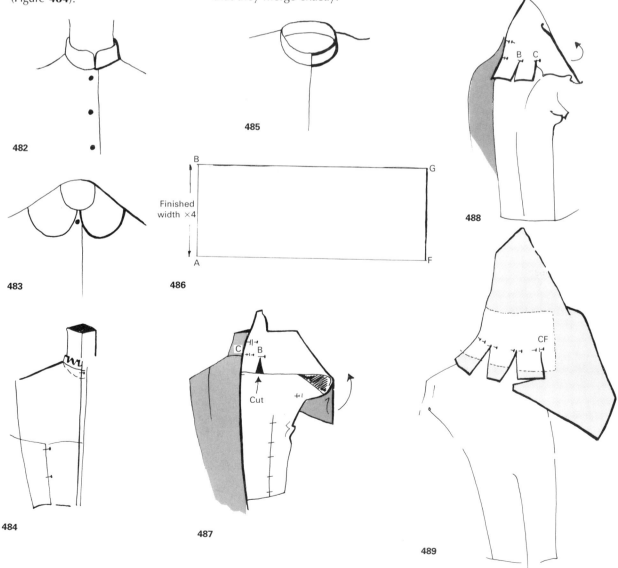

482

483

484

485

Finished width ×4

486

487

488

489

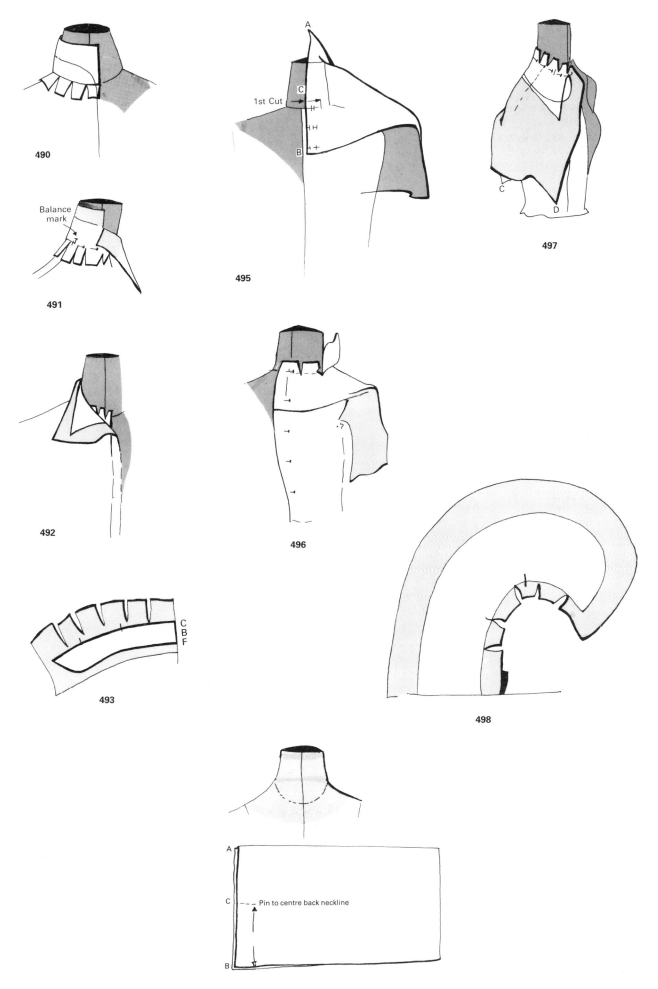

490

491
Balance mark

492

493
C
B
F

494
A
C · - - - Pin to centre back neckline
B

495
A
C
1st Cut
B

496

497
C
D

498

FLAT GROWN-ON COLLAR
Flat sailor collar (Figure 499)

1 Take the basic front bodice block and lay it face downwards with the selvedge parallel to the centre front (Figure **500**).
2 Mark around from **C–A–B** (Figure **500**). **D** is halfway down the centre front.
3 Add **A** from **D** plus 10 cm (Figure **501**).
4 Remove the block from the fabric.
5 Mirror the shoulder angle from line **E–F** for the first cut (Figure **501**).
6 Cut to point **C** (Figure **501**).
7 Point **C** can be either placed to the neck point or away from it according to style.
8 Position point **C** to the neck point of the stand (Figure **502**).
9 Model in the front bodice (Figure **503**).
10 Fold over and lay the fabric into position over the body to the given break point (Figure **503**).

Figure **504** illustrates the front collar with the breakline.

11 Trim away the excess fabric.
12 Cut into the centre front break point and open out the button stand.

Fischu collar with drapes arranged from the front part of the collar (Figure 507).

A bow can be added if desired. The modelled collar is in fact the under collar and there will be a seam in the centre back. The top collar (Figure **508**) is the facing, and, to remove the need for a seam down the centre back, place the centre back on the fold. Place on to the straight grain and allow for 'pressing under' all the way down the leaf edge. Model the rest of the bodice as for the previous bodice.

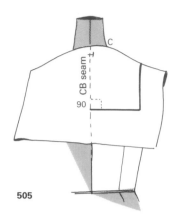

505

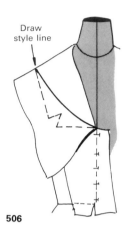

506

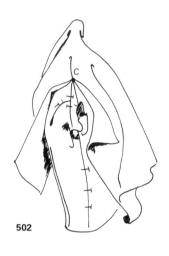

502

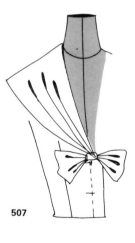

507

499

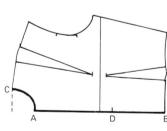

500

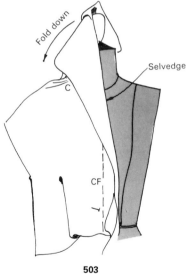

503

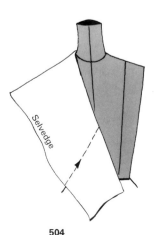

504

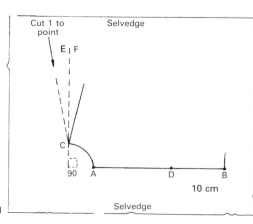

501

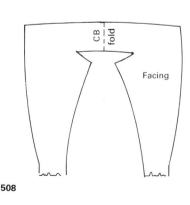

508

GROWN-ON COLLAR WITH STAND

The same principles apply to this collar as the previous collar. Cut the fabric as before by marking the centre front, points and angles. See Figure **501**.

Figure **509** illustrates the collar. Follow exactly Figure **501** by arranging that the centre front is on the straight grain.

1 Mark the centre front and the break point (Figures **511** and **512**).
2 Trim away as the diagram and model the dart at the waist (Figure **511**).
3 The break point is a pivot to be used to ascertain the amount of collar stand.
4 Hold the centre front down with a pin (Figures **511** and **512**).
5 Place a hand under the collar and determine the amount of stand required at the shoulder neck point.
6 Holding that measurement, trace the collar around to the centre back (Figure **513**).
7 Define the amount of collar stand (Figure **513**).
8 Trim away the unwanted fabric and nip into the neck ring (Figure **514**).
9 Cut into the suggested leaf edge of the collar to reduce the points of stress and adjust the stand at the centre back to reduce stress in the stand by raising the back neck upwards.

The Jenny collar (Figure 516)

This collar frames the face; it is wide, bold and very versatile. The collar could have a centre back seam if a stripe or check fabric is used to form a chevron. If a plain weave is used, the collar may be cut in one piece.

1 Fold and cut the fabric (Figure **517**). Figure **518** illustrates the open fabric.
2 The prepared bodice (Figure **519**). Plan the back and front neck line as required, with pins.
3 Decide the approximate width of the collar and place the folded fabric on to the collar line and place pins to stabilize the fabric at the centre front (Figure **520**). Figure **521** shows the back view.
4 Cut up along and into the line of pins (Figure **522**).
5 A stand will begin to appear at the neck (Figure **523**).
6 Continue cutting into the pinned neckline and working the collar around the neck until the desired appearance is obtained (Figure **523**).
7 Ensure that the leaf edge is not cramped (Figure **523**). Adjust the collar width by removing pins from the centre front to two-thirds the way up to the shoulder and realign the collar to desired width. Position balance marks and mark along the line of pins to establish the neckline of bodice and collar neckline.

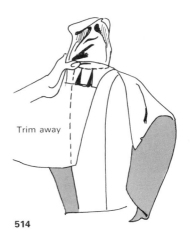

Trim away

514

Use a seam on the CB of under collar and facing

515

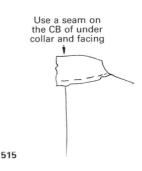

Stand
Fall

516

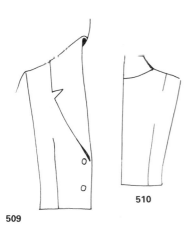

509

510

512

Break point

CF1

513

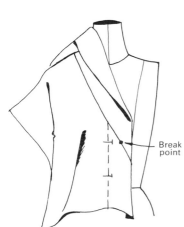

Break point

511

Selvedge
CB
Stand
Fall
Fold
Cut
Cut
Cut

517

CB
Straight grain

518

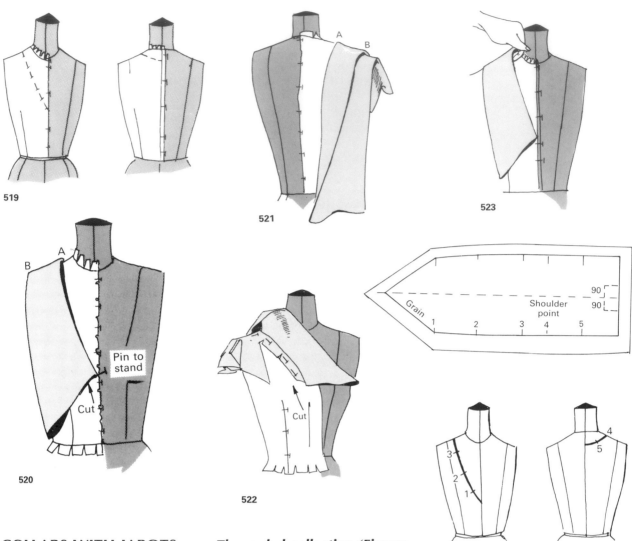

519

521

523

520

522

COLLARS WITH JABOTS

The following styles depict the fashion of many years ago and have a basic timeless quality. They are created by formula and direct drafting methods and are very good examples of shapes within shapes. A great deal is to be learned from the techniques used to achieve their shapes, and, after some practice using the printed dimensions, the shapes of the pieces will hopefully imprint themselves on the toilist's mind. Draft these patterns as illustrated and apply them to the desired area of the dress stand. It is also recommended that various proportions are tried and evaluated. Eventually these pieces will be produced freehand by the toilist and integrated into the garment. It is at this stage that 'shape within shape' becomes meaningful and the triangle cut on the true bias can be seen to contain the cowl effect whilst a triangle cut on the straight can be seen to contain a fluted jabot effect.

It is the use of imagination coupled with the feel for the three-dimension that will lead from the rather tight and stuffy but charming exercises on this page to virtually anywhere within the field of the productively wearable garment.

The rochal collection (Figures 524 to 531)

Draft these styles on to paper or directly on to fabric. Note that the dimensions are approximate and can be varied according to the proportions of the garment.

Figures **532** to **535** show details of the cowl collar and roll collar.

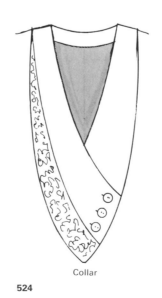

524

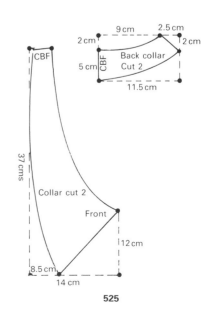

525

526

Collar with jobot

527

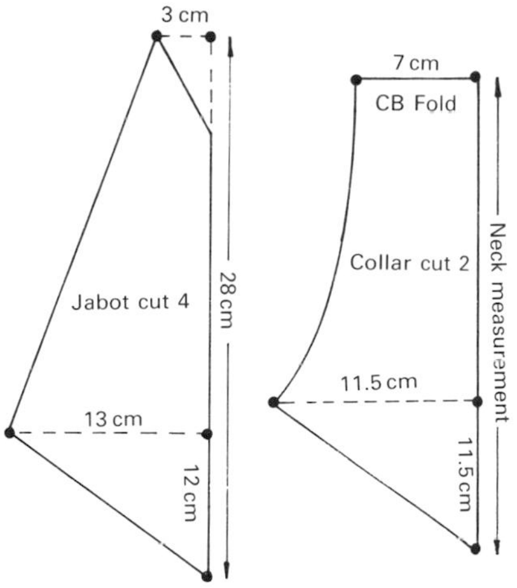

3 cm

Jabot cut 4

28 cm

13 cm

12 cm

7 cm

CB Fold

Collar cut 2

Neck measurement

11.5 cm

11.5 cm

528

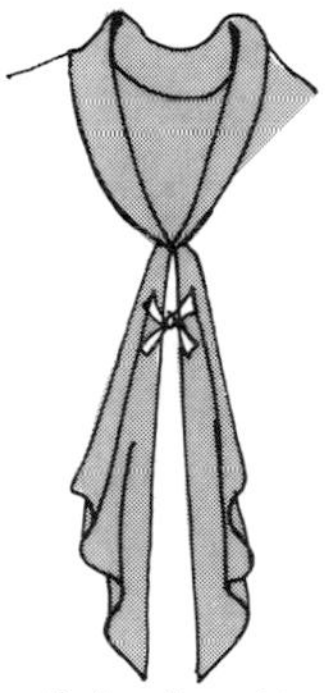

Roll collar with jabot

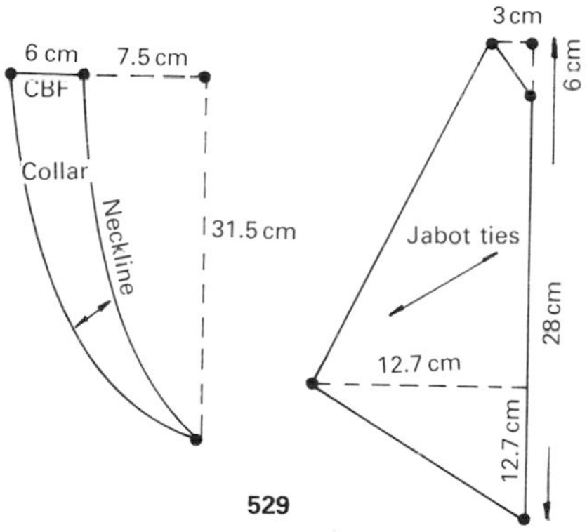

529

6 cm

CBF

Collar

Neckline

31.5 cm

7.5 cm

3 cm

6 cm

Jabot ties

12.7 cm

28 cm

12.7 cm

530

531

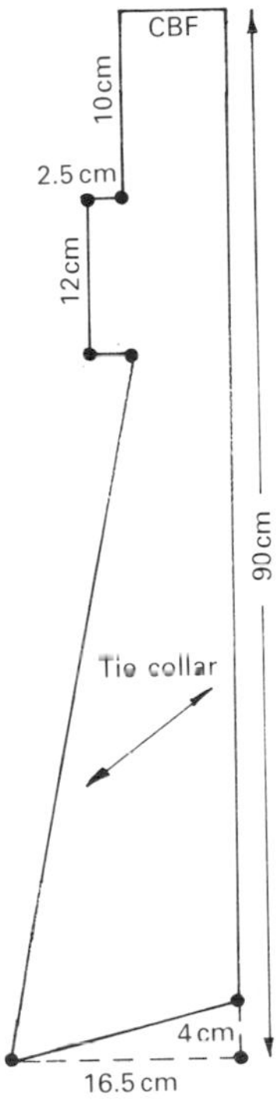

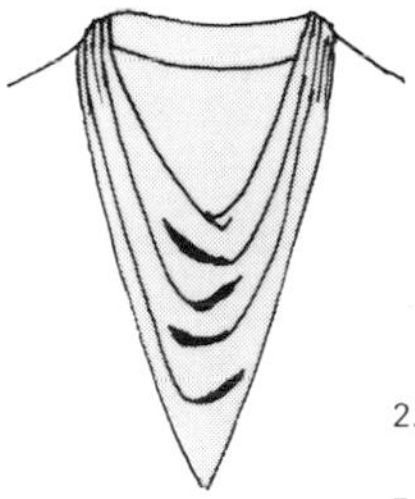

CBF

10 cm

2.5 cm

12 cm

90 cm

Tie collar

4 cm

16.5 cm

532

Cowl collar

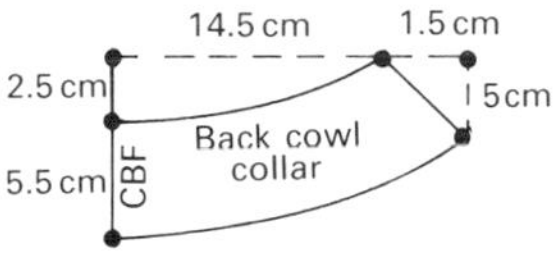

533

14.5 cm

1.5 cm

2.5 cm

CBF

Back cowl collar

5.5 cm

5 cm

7.5 cm

30.0 cm

2 cm

5 cm

Cowl collar

CFF

Grain

35.5 cm

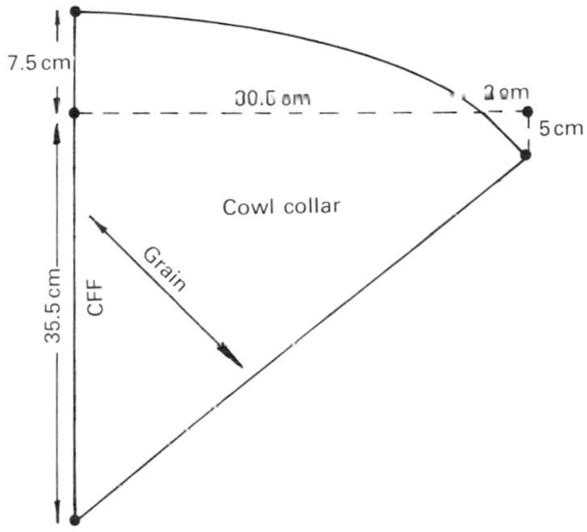

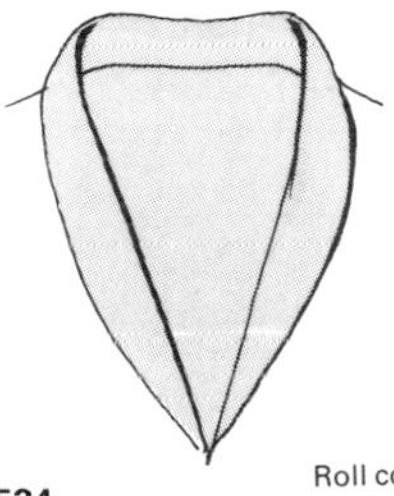

534

Roll collar

535

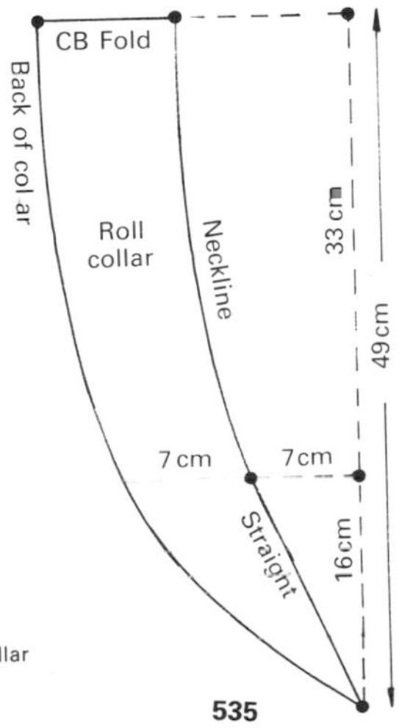

CB Fold

Back of collar

Roll collar

Neckline

Straight

33 cm

49 cm

7 cm

7 cm

16 cm

THE SIMPLE COWL

The simple cowl (Figure **536**) in many respects is the purest of modelling styles. To obtain the full beauty of this style the correct fabric and grain must be carefully considered. Ideally this style should be draped from a soft knitted fabric like silk jersey, but in practice almost any soft knitted or woven fabric can be used successfully.

1. Cut a 90 cm square fabric and halve, it diagonally (Figure **537**).
2. Cut off the triangle (Figure **538**).
3. Finger fold and finger press the fabric (Figure **539**).
4. Open out the fabric and mark the centre bias **A−B** (Figure **542**).
5. Reverse over the fabric and fold back 4 cm to nothing causing a curve on the fold (Figure **540**).
6. Fold again (Figure **531**). A cowl is caused by two collisions, i.e. extra fabric width colliding with extra fabric length.
7. Decide on the finished width of the shoulders and how much back will be exposed (Figure **541**).
8. Position pins **C** to **E** to judge the depth from centre back.
9. Mark fabric **A−B−C** (Figure **542**).
10. Pick up **C**1 and pin to **C**1 on the stand (Figure **543**).
11. Use the palm of the hand to create a pivot whereby the fabric is pulled around under stress to cause a line and tension for the top fold (Figure **544**).
12. The cowl should be balanced and setting over the centre back (Figure **545**).

THE FOLDS

Note that the weft will react differently from the warp when the folds are picked up.

1. Lift up the quantity of fabric on the **C**2 side located in the centre drape (Figure **545**).
2. Space out the folds and quantity and then test each fold for depth and strength.
3. Continue picking up fabric and forming the cowls until the desired effect is achieved (Figures **546**−**548**).
4. Trim and insert or suspend as design requires.

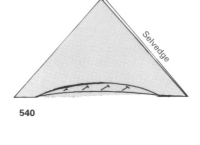

540

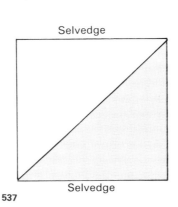

Selvedge

Selvedge

537

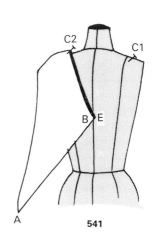

541

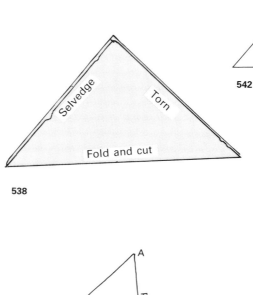

Selvedge

Torn

Fold and cut

538

Fold

539

542

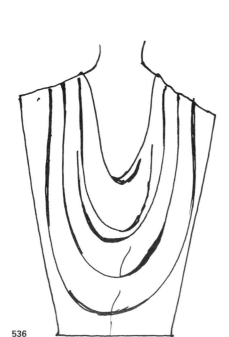

536

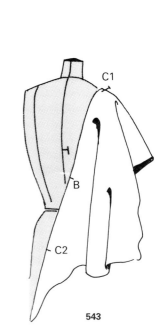

543

544

545

546

547

548

THE STRAPLESS BODICE

This strapless bodice (Figure **549**) forms the basis of many of the fitted evening-wear garments worn today. Although it is by definition very contour hugging, it should at no time be tight and stressed against the body. If the bodice is too tight, the body will try to escape, usually over the top! If the strapless bodice is well boned and constructed it will eliminate the need to wear an undergarment. This garment has an element of corsetry about it.

1 Measure off a length of fabric from the centre front neck to below the waist. The width of the fabric will be determined by the width of centre front to bust point plus 8 cm (Figure **550**).
2 Pin the straight grain of the fabric selvedge way down to the centre front of the stand (Figure **551**).
3 Place a pin parallel to the bust point so that fabric can be folded back (Figure **551**).
4 Fold back the fabric to expose the bust point (Figure **552**).
5 Position the side section of the fabric on to the side section of the stand and pin to secure to the body (Figures **553** and **554**).
6 Grip the two sections together (Figure **555**).
7 Pin to the bust point (Figure **556**).
8 Pin along the contour of the seam. Whilst pinning, watch what is happening on the centre section (Figure **556**).
9 Figure **557** illustrates the centre front section and the stress points.
10 Remove the pins from the bust point upwards (Figure **558**).
11 Pivot from the bust point downwards to form a dart at centre front (Figure **558**).
12 Pin to the centre front (Figure **558**).
13 Pin from below the waistline upwards, feeling the contour of the diaphragm (Figures **559** and **560**).
14 Pass the excess fabric upwards until the between bosom area is reached and pass the excess fabric into the already formed dart (Figures **559** and **560**).
15 Redraw the centre front which should no longer be a straight line (Figures **559** and **560**).

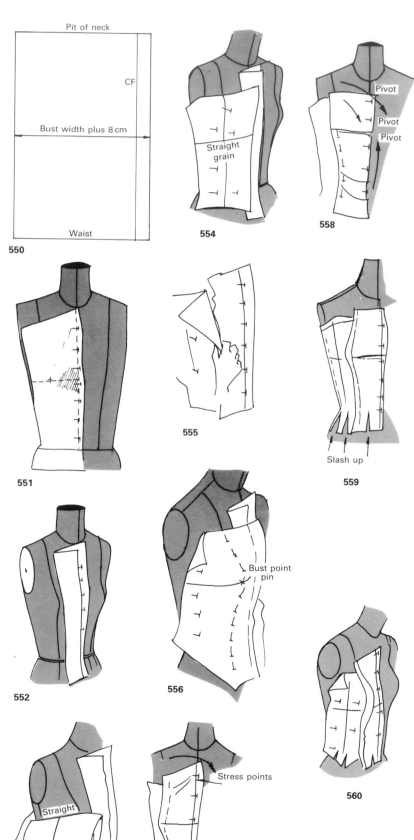

550

554

558

551

555

559 Slash up

552

556 Bust point pin

560

553 Straight

557 Stress points / Stress point

549   Fitted bodice

The back

1 Take a rectangle of fabric measuring approximately in length from across back to just below the waist, and pin down to the back as illustrated (Figure **561**).
2 Pivot the fabric gently around from the centre back to the waist (Figure **562**).
3 Draw the dart together and settle over the contour of back body so that the top of the dart is under the blade (Figure **562**).
4 Trim away the excess fabric from the side seam.
5 Join the side seam back bodice to front bodice (Figure **563**).
6 Place the first pin at the bust point level at the side seam.

Figure **564** shows the side view.

7 Position a tape along the chest around the back and mark along the top of the tape. Trim away to the nearest 2 cm (Figure **564**).
8 Pass excess fullness from the side seam into a small dart about 3 cm from the bust point (Figure **565**).
9 Mark up the seams along the pinned line.
10 Place balance marks where necessary.

This will serve as a foundation for the following styles.

THE CLASSIC RUCHED BODICE (FIGURES 566 AND 567)

1 Prepare the strapless foundation and bone the bodice as required.
2 Cut the fabric on the exact bias (Figure **568**).
3 Measure from the centre front to the waist multiplied by two and a half times to calculate the length of fabric required (Figure **568**). This calculation is based on a reasonably firm but light fabric. If a chiffon is used, be prepared to estimate up to four times that measurement. If velvet is used, use less than two and a half times.
4 Locate the centre front and sew a tacking thread using a 1 cm stitch (Figure **569**).
5 Draw up the gathering thread to the centre front length required and fasten over a pin (Figure **569**).
6 Position on to the dress stand with pins at 2 cm intervals. Adjust quantity of gathering at this point (Figure **570**).
7 Locate the bust point and place a second line of gathering thread (Figure **571**).
8 Draw up the second line of gathering and pin through on to the under bodice (Figure **571**).
9 Continue gathering and pinning in this manner on all the body construction lines as they are reached until finally ending at the centre back (Figure **572**).
10 All surplus fabric will exit via the centre back as the bodice becomes shorter from the side seam to the CM. Keep waist straight, but pass surplus ruche up and out of the top of the bodice.

563

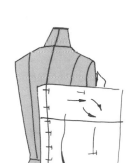

561

562

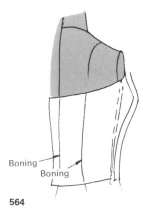

Boning
Boning

564

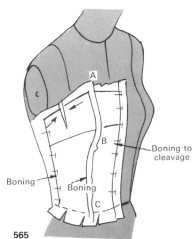

A
B
C
Boning to cleavage
Boning
Boning

565

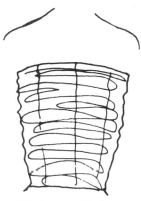

566   Classic ruched bodice

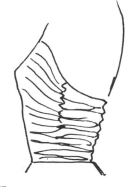

567

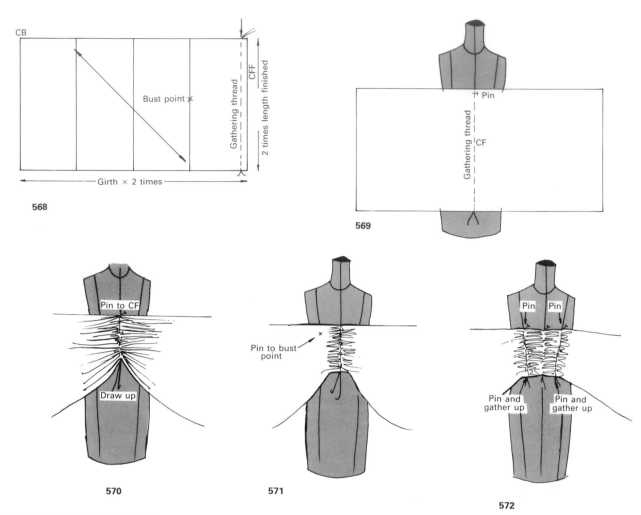

568

569

570

571

572

THE FIGURE EIGHT BODICE (FIGURE 573)

1 Prepare the strapless bodice as before, boned and ready for its cladding.
2 Place pins into the bust points (Figure **574**).
3 The amount of fabric required will be based on the measurement of side seam to side seam plus about 10 cm (Figure **575**).
4 Fold the fabric and lightly finger crease about half way down (Figure **576**).
5 Turn down about a quarter of the length and finger crease (Figure **577**).
6 Open out the fabric and mark in lightly the creased cruciform (Figure **578**).
7 Mark the centre front position (Figure **578**).
8 Position the fabric into the fitted bodice foundation and pin the centre front and immediately locate and pin the bust points (BP) (Figure **579**).
9 Remove the original pins under markers. *Note* that the straight grain is between the bust points.

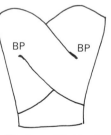

The figure fitted bodice

573

574

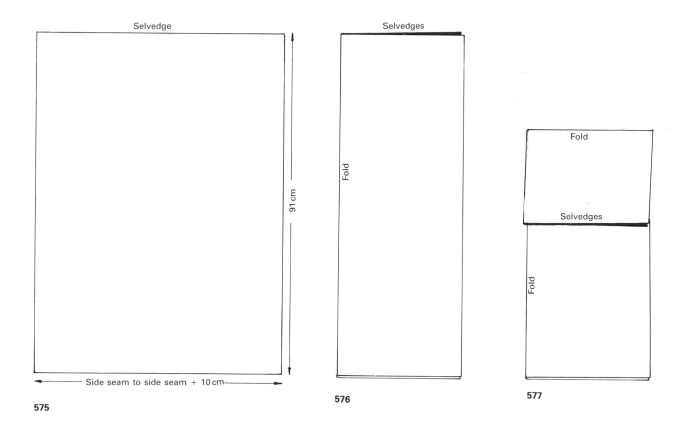

Selvedge

91 cm

Side seam to side seam + 10 cm

575

Selvedges

Fold

576

Fold

Selvedges

Fold

577

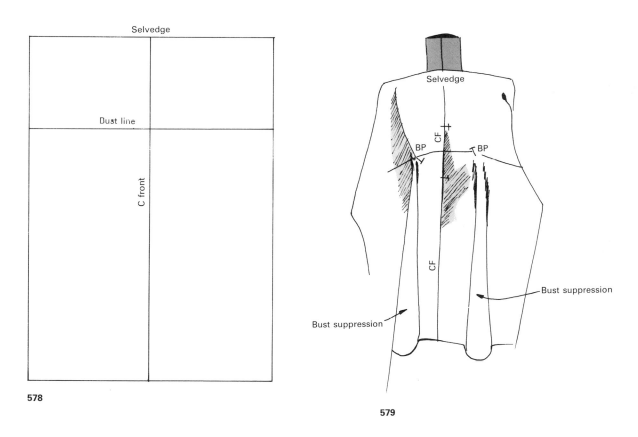

Selvedge

Dust line

C front

578

Selvedge

CF

BP   BP

CF

Bust suppression

Bust suppression

579

Suppression

At this stage the bodice suppression is positioned into approximate areas for the later stage of styling.

1 Sweep fabric around so that the bust suppression below the bust point is manipulated from the bust point pin to the above the bust point and is now in readiness to be placed into its correct angle (Figures **580** and **581**.

Dart lines

1 Place a row of pins so that the **A–B** measurement equals **C–D** (Figure **582**).
2 Release any tensions that can be found and marry the top to the under bodice (Figure **582**).
3 Adjust the line of pins so that it is the edge of the folded suppression (Figure **583**).
4 Place a row of pins to mirror the centre front to side seam. Cut away the shaded area (Figure **583**).
5 Cut from the waist to the proximity of the lower line of pins (Figure **584**).
6 Raise the lower line of pins and sweep the suppression under the line of pins (Figure **584**).
7 Cut away the unwanted fabric (Figure **585**).

Figure **586** shows the finished bodice and Figure **587** the open shape.

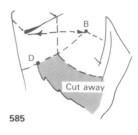

585

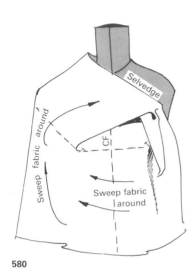

580

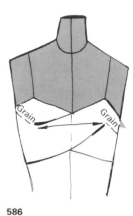

586

581

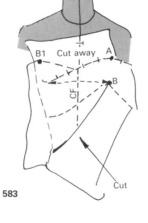

583

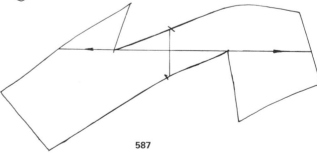

587

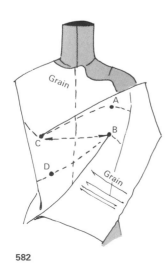

582

584

General size chart

Body measurements for medium bust development:
Increments are based on an increase of 5 cm girth and 2.4 cm height.

	Area	10	12	14	16	18	20	22	Increment
1	Height	159.6	162.0	164.4	166.8	169.2	171.6	174.0	2.4
2	Weight (Pounds)	102	118	134	150	166	182	198	16lb
3	Hip	87.0	92.0	97.0	102.0	107.0	112.0	117.0	5.0
4	Bust	81.0	86.0	91.0	96.0	101.0	106.0	111.0	5.0
5	Waist	61.0	66.0	71.0	76.0	81.0	86.0	91.0	5.0
6	Chest	77.4	81.0	84.6	88.2	91.8	95.4	99.0	3.6
7	Top hip (11 cm from waist)	81.0	86.0	91.0	96.0	101.0	106.0	111.0	5.0
8	Rib cage (under bust)	66.0	71.0	76.0	81.0	86.0	91.0	96.0	5.0
9	Neck	35.0	36.0	37.0	38.0	39.0	40.0	41.0	1.0
10	Bicep	24.7	26.5	28.3	30.1	31.9	33.7	35.5	1.8
11	Elbow	23.7	25.5	27.3	29.1	30.9	32.7	34.5	1.8
12	Wrist	15.2	16.0	16.8	17.6	18.4	19.2	20.0	0.8
13	Thigh	49.8	53.0	56.2	59.4	62.6	65.8	69.0	3.2
14	Knee	32.6	34.0	35.4	36.8	38.2	39.6	41.0	1.4
15	Calf	31.6	33.0	34.4	35.8	37.2	38.6	40.0	1.4
16	Ankle	22.3	23.0	23.7	24.4	25.1	25.8	26.5	0.7
17	X−chest	29.8	31.0	32.2	33.4	34.6	35.8	37.0	1.2
18	X−back (12 cm down from nape)	31.8	33.0	34.2	35.4	36.6	37.8	39.0	1.2
19	Shoulder length	11.7	11.9	12.1	12.3	12.5	12.7	12.9	0.2
20	Scye width	10.1	11.0	11.9	12.8	13.7	14.6	15.5	0.9
21	Scye depth	17.5	18.1	18.7	19.3	19.9	20.5	21.1	0.6
22	Bust width	17.8	19.0	20.2	21.4	22.6	23.8	25.0	1.2
23	Nape to bust	32.6	34.0	35.4	36.8	38.2	39.6	41.0	1.4
24	Nape to waist over bust	51.8	53.0	54.2	55.4	56.6	57.8	59.0	1.2
25	Nape to waist centre back	40.4	41.0	41.6	42.2	42.8	43.4	44.0	0.6
26	Nape to hip	62.1	63.0	63.9	64.8	65.7	66.6	67.5	0.9
27	Nape to knee	97.5	99.0	100.5	102.0	103.5	105.0	106.5	1.5
28	Nape to floor	137.9	140.0	142.1	144.2	146.3	148.4	150.5	2.1
29	Sleeve length (outer)	57.1	58.0	58.9	59.8	60.7	61.6	62.5	0.9
30	Sleeve length (inner)	43.1	43.5	43.9	44.3	44.7	45.1	45.5	0.4
31	Abdominal seat diameter	21.3	23.0	24.7	26.4	28.1	29.8	31.5	1.7
32	Hip width	30.2	31.8	33.4	35.0	36.6	38.2	39.8	1.6
33	Body rise	27.9	29.0	30.1	31.2	32.3	33.4	34.5	1.1
34	Shoulder angle (degrees)	20.5	20.5	20.5	20.5	20.5	20.5	20.5	NIL
35	Outside leg	100.5	102.0	103.5	105.0	106.5	108.0	109.5	1.5

FURTHER READING

M.M. Shoben and J.P. Ward, *Pattern Cutting and Making Up, the Professional Approach* (Heinemann Professional Publishing 1987)

M.M. Shoben and J.P. Ward *Pattern Cutting and Making Up for outerwear Fashions* (Heinemann Professional Publishing 1990)

M.M. Shoben *Patterns from your Favourite Clothes,* (Heinemann Professional Publishing 1988)

M.M. Shoben, *Short Cut to Fashion* (Hutchinson 1985)

P.J. Taylor and M.M. Shoben *Grading for the Fashion Industry* (Stanley Thorns Publishers 1990)

SUPPLIERS

Calico-Net-Silks,
Whaleys (Bradford) Ltd
Harris Court,
Great Horton,
Bradford,
West Yorkshire BD7 4E0

Morplan, Garment Trade Supplies
Service,
56, Great Titchfield St,
London W1P 8 DX

R.D. Franks Ltd
Kent House,
Market Place,
Oxford Circus,
London W1P 8DY

LONDON
centre
for
FASHION
STUDIES

London Centre
for
Fashion Studies
Day, evening and Saturday classes
for all levels
From beginners to advanced

● Design ● Fashion illustration ●
● Pattern cutting ● Grading ●
For women's, men's and children's wear

Courses individually designed.
Send now for a prospectus and
enrolment form to:

Martin Shoben, MA BEd, FCFI
23 Bevenden Street, London N1 6BN
Tel: 071−490−7357

Index

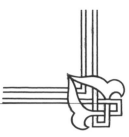

Asymmetrical dress, 28—30

Ball, 82
Ball sleeve, 82
Bias tight fitting, 79
 sleeve, 79
Brandy glass skirt, 67
Bridal trains, 38—43
Bridalwear, 35—49
 concepts, 36
 fabrics, 36
 planning, 36
 sleeves, 36
Bows:
 ends, 46
 flat, three piece bias cut, 44—5
Bust suppression, 54

Cha Cha frill, 34
Circles, full, quarter, half, 72—3
Circle cutting, principles, 72—5
Circular effects, 73—5
Classic ruched bodice, 97—8
Cleopatra drape, 22—4
Collars, 88—93
 with jabots, 92—3
Contour, 3
Cowls, 80—1, 94—5
 collar, 93
 natural, 81
 sleeves, 80—1

Darts:
 French, 63
 manipulation, 62—3
 multiple, 63—5
 principles, 62—4
 waist, 63
Dhoti:
 with displaced seam, 12
 with inside seam, 10
Dress, sheath, 70—1
Dress stand, 53
Dress with handkerchief hem, 25—7
Dolman sleeve, 86—7

Ethnic trousers, 10—14

Fabrics, 5
 knitted, 5
 knitted rib, 5
 woven, 5
Figure of eight bodice, 9
Fischu collar with drapes, 90
Fitted bodice, 96—7
Flared skirts, 65—6
Flat grown on collar, 90
Flowers, simple rosette, snail rose, 47
Four-panelled double circle skirt,
 32—3
Front bodice, 53—4
Full circle, 72
Full circle skirts, 66
Full dhoti, 13—14

Godets, 74—5
Great knott, 15—18
Grown on collar with stand, 91

Half circle, 73
Half dhoti, 10

Jenny collar, 91—3

Lattice sleeve, 83—6
Levelling skirts, 66

Modelling, basic skills, 50—100

Natural cowl sleeve, 81

One-piece side-draped skirt, 19—21
Onion or windswept look, 8, 9

Padded arm, 76
Peg top shape skirt, 67
Peter Pan collar, 88—9
Puff ball, 6

Quarter circle, 72

Rochal collection, 92—3
Roll collar, 93
 with jabot, 93

Seamlines, 3
Sheath dress, 70—1
Skirts:
 double circular, 30
 flared, 65—6
 four panelled with double circle,
  32—3
 full circle, 66
 levelling, 66
 modelling the block, 57—9
 peg top and brandy glass shape, 67
 side draped, 19—21
 threaded drape, 31—3
 wrap-over drape and waterfall,
  68—9
Size chart, 101
Sleeves, 76—87
 cha cha, 34
 lattice, 83—6
 straight, 76—7
 straight sleeve with elbow dart,
  76—8
Souffle skirt, 7
Stand or Mandarin collar, 88—9
Strapless bodice, 96—100
Surface decoration, 44—8

Threaded drape skirt, 31—3
Toiles, 3
 evaluation, 3, 60—1
 making, 5
Trains:
 combined with bow, 41—3
 detachable, 38—9
 kite shape, 39—40

Veils, full length, the square veil,
 48—9

Waist suppression, 54
Waistbands, 10
Waterfall drape, 68—9
Wrap-over, bias cut dress, 22—4
Wrap-over drape and waterfall, 68—9